D1139215

Crime Chemist

ALAN DOWER

Crime Chemist

The Life Story of Charles Anthony Taylor Scientist for the Crown

JOHN LONG *London*

JOHN LONG LIMITED
178-202 Great Portland Street, London, W.1

London Melbourne Sydney
Auckland Bombay Toronto
Johannesburg New York

First published 1965

This book has been set in Baskerville, printed in Great Britain on Antique Wove paper by Cheltenham Press Ltd., Cheltenham and bound by Wm. Brendon & Son Ltd., Tiptree, Essex.

Contents

Illustrations

Between pages 88 and 89

Foreword 1

By CHARLES ANTHONY TAYLOR
B.Sc A.A.C.I

NOTHING less than a huge compendium could possibly hold every detail of any Government Analyst's official life and the investigations of almost formidable variety that are passed his way or so often gladly unburdened at his feet.

But here – assembled by one who knew me well and who inherited and extended an extraordinary police and crime-investigating background – is a selection of specimens to leave a record of an analyst's trials and challenges. I understand it is the first time that this particular field has been explored and its tales chronicled by an Australian writer.

Through my thirty or so years as Government Analyst, I averaged an important or intriguing case at least five times each month and sometimes every second day. The subject matter might range from cognac, cocaine, ammonia, morphine and opium or herbal remedies to possums, fur coats, tongues, fish and sausage.

The work of a Government Analyst keeps him on his toes physically and mentally day and night. In my case, I had to trek into some of the most remote corners of the Australian bush and – as in the case of the Royal Commission on Sanitation in 1926 – to Lismore, Murwillumbah and Sydney in New South Wales, and Toowoomba and Brisbane in Queensland, some 1,000 miles away.

As others have found, it was a task with great difficulties, but it offered the great reward of helping to bring the guilty men to justice. It was a full and satisfying life – one that I would live again. It required patience and endurance and often an abundant sense of humour.

Behind me I had a devoted wife who, while she raised six children, gave that sturdy confidence and support that enabled the grimmest problem to be attacked with at least resolution.

Frequently with me in the field were police whose friendship and memory I respect. The author's father, big Robert John Dower, was a CIB Chief of physique and intellect, who unfailingly gave me a straight go clearly and honestly right down the line.

They were a very kind and warm and thoughtful crowd, these police. And calm and penetrating, too. Men like Charles Petty, with whom I once had the privilege to work during his junior days, and who became Deputy-Commissioner of Police.

I had the advantage, too, of having studied some of the medical degree subjects during my university training in science. This – and my earlier experiences on goldfields and even school-teaching for the pittance of five shillings a week – gave me a background that proved priceless.

To the young man coming up I urge attention to the harvesting of all knowledge, no matter how trivial or irrelevant it may seem. His field will remain enormous, especially in this far-reaching nuclear age. The bracket of problems this alone has introduced must bear heavily on him.

As I see it at the age of seventy-nine, his position may not be eased by one important change that seems to have come over the medico-legal field since I and my colleagues retired. Throughout our years the independence of the official scientist was never doubted or questioned. The same independence in his own qualified right applied to the Government pathologist – men like the late Dr Crawford Mollison. Each had his own indisputable charter. Each was master in his different yet related field – one in forensic science, the other in forensic medicine. Individually they were specialists. Together, whenever the need arose – and that was often – they were a powerful combination.

Now, unhappily, I believe forensic science has been brought

too close to medicine. There is a danger that the individualities of both may be lost in the compounding, that pure science and its experts may lose part of their original charter by being sublimated or subordinated to the influence of medicine.

Alan Dower, however, rightly has not attempted to gaze into the crystal ball. Like the pure scientist, he has confined his picture strictly to the hard facts of an era that has just closed, and the like of which – because of the incredibly fast-changing and confusing times – will not be seen again.

Foreword 2

By ALEX M. DUNCAN, C.M.G J.P
Former Chief Commissioner of Police in State of Victoria, Australia; former Chief of the Scotland Yard Flying Squad; member of Interpol.

WHEN I first arrived in Australia, twenty-eight years ago, it was at the invitation of the Government of Victoria to investigate and report on the overall structure and future of the Police Force of that State. A Royal Commission had recommended an inquiry of this nature after investigating certain matters which gave rise to public disquiet concerning the Police Service.

My police appointment in the London Metropolitan Police at that time was Chief Detective-Inspector of the Flying Squad, Scotland Yard. I left Britain with many years of police experience behind me and – as it turned out – with many more ahead, making an aggregate of forty-four years' service on my retirement from active duties.

Those years in Britain had been interesting, instructive, memorable and satisfying; sometimes hard and tiring, but always exciting. I had the honour of working closely with, and knowing many talented personalities whose dedication and example inspired me, and so often disproved the old adage that a policeman's life is not a happy one.

Among these were John Horwell, George Cornish, Hugh Young, Fred Cherrill, all brilliant Yard officers; the late Sir Bernard Spilsbury, Dr Roche Lynch, and Cyril Cuthbert in the science field. In another field was that unforgettable personality the late Edgar Wallace, and my good and amusing friend Sir Harry Lauder. My association with these two soon convinced me of the great public appetite and interest in police affairs.

As the years passed and my horizons extended, new faces came into focus, bringing with them everlasting friendships with such people as Willie Merrilees, for many years in charge of the detective force of Edinburgh City Police, and now Chief Constable of Scotland's Lothian and Peebles Constabulary, a remarkable policeman with a great will and capacity for helping a lame dog over a stile.

It is understandable that my thoughts were mixed when I reached the vast continent of Australia. Some folk possibly were suspicious of me, others full of curiosity. I soon found that there were many redoubtedly open friends. I found, too – something still not understood completely overseas – how the structure and character of an Australian State Police Force does and must vary from those abroad. The Australian forces are sovereign bodies within the States, and they are responsible for the maintenance of law and order within their States – some covering an area of more than half a million square miles. There are no County, City, or Borough Forces, as in Britain. The lonely constable in the far 'outback' country, therefore, and his loyal and indispensable wife – how much I credit her! – has territorial, social and civic responsibilities and trials through flood, bushfire, drought and crime waves that cannot always be fully understood elsewhere.

My initial travels through the far country on investigations engendered in me a great admiration for grand police work being done, and for the Australian way of life. On the other hand, it was obvious that reforms and expansions must be strongly recommended. One was a reconstruction of the Criminal Investigation Branch then centralised in the city, a reshuffle with some deployment to key country areas. During my reconnaissance period I met many men of outstanding ability who were most helpful. Two come to mind – Arthur Webster, who in later years became my deputy, and Robert John Dower, father of the author of this book, who was in charge of the Criminal Investigation Branch of the Force till his retirement.

As Alan Dower points out, communications and mobility

over vast distances were originally much more limited than today, but enterprise, resourcefulness and energy were there in abundance. When World War Two was on us, we had on the drawing board plans for a duplicate communication system – D.24, as it was known – a long-range radio hook-up which proved most effective.

When peace came we quickly realised the need to link strongly with the Interpol organisation, which of course had ceased to operate during the war years. It was my honour to attend the International Criminal Police Commission in 1947 and have Australia accepted as a full member and I became the Commission's Australian representative.

Inside our force other changes and advancements were made. A detective training college was established. A police officers' college was mooted, and the scientific bureau was further developed. A fascinating new method of transmitting finger-print ciphers was perfected, and initial plans were discussed by myself and the then Commissioner in London. The final technique was perfected by two of the world's leading finger-print experts, Superintendent Cherrill of the Yard and Inspector (later Superintendent) Alec Martin of my force. This system was announced in Melbourne in 1945. Some time later, using the new technique, Martin was responsible for the capture in Australia of a criminal who had slunk into the country with cleverly forged documents after having served terms of imprisonment in England, Europe and South Africa, for crimes committed in New South Wales.

Another officer who gave good service in his field was Inspector Fred Hobley, who was first chief of our scientific bureau. Such men – and of course others in the homicide and similar specialist squads – had very warm, trusting and effective working relationships with specialists outside our department and yet within its working orbit. One was the capable Government pathologist, Dr Crawford Mollison, and another the medico-legal chemist, Mr Charles Anthony Taylor.

The strength of any police department is in the sum of the wise yet practical people it retains in its own right, and their staunch allies in the specialists' fields. The famous Constable Gutteridge murder case in Essex in 1927 – in which I had the good fortune, with a Liverpool detective, to overpower one of the two murderers, Kennedy – had never left me with any inhibitions about calling on any person, or dredging up any scrap of information, to help solve a crime.

By the same maxim, all possible knowledge and experience – yet without a melodramatic and exaggerated concentration – must be focused sharply on a crime spot with absolute minimum delay. That was our *modus operandi* at the Yard – police, pathologist, chemist, photographer, fingerprint expert, draftsman and so on taking the field as a co-ordinated unit. The same principles are followed in Australia's Victoria Force, which I knew and admired so much.

Mr Taylor as Government Analyst, and Dr Mollison as Government pathologist, were often leading members of that crime-fighting team. They earned the greatest respect from my officers and men – especially through the more difficult years when faith, fortitude and even philosophy had to be the great allies of craftsmanship and science. Like those who shared our policeman's lot in war and peace, they earned our salutes and thanks.

Whilst serving as Commissioner of Police in Victoria it was my privilege to become acquainted with Alan Dower. He was then, for about fifteen years, chief crime reporter for a leading Melbourne daily paper, *The Herald*, and has specialised in the crime field since. I have always cherished a high regard for him over the years and have appreciated his many courtesies in those days.

Author's Introduction

No criminal of Australia ever belled 'The Cat' and none of the many riddles showered on him remained unsolved. In this decade he might be called the real cool man of crime, one who did not lose a case through thirty years and whose evidence was never thrown from court.

As a scientist he was great because his knowledge truly was prodigious and his powers of reasoning were superb. As a sleuth he was a giant because he flatly refused to admit defeat, and proved by his tenacity that even the most exasperating and evasive problem could be solved. As a witness he was unshakably supreme. Above all, he became a dedicated man.

Once he was an unsettled boy from the big, hot Australian bush. But he became the nation's Bernard Spilsbury.

Charles Anthony Taylor is his name, which rang so often through the highest courts in Australia.

It was inevitable, perhaps, that in the world which knew his sagacity and skill he became 'The Cat.' Not only because his initials ran that way, but because he carefully stalked before he sprang or pounced. And because 'the eyes' always had it!

They were piercing, penetrating, half-closed, blue-grey eyes that windowed a well-stocked, orderly and calculating brain. That was always the first and enduring impression of the man who had fossicked for gold specks on worn-out minefields as a kid, and grew up as the formidable seeker and sworn valuer of the deadly trifles that so often give criminals away.

Because he and I have spent so much of our lives on police affairs, I have chosen to recapture and write of several of his triumphs on a windy hill that broods over Melbourne and the downtown canyons of stone that once were the shallow valleys where the aborigines fished and roamed.

It is Russell Street hill, and it is not the city's nicest. It is battered by the howling south-westerlies of winter and beaten by the roasting northerlies of summer. It seems arid and spiritless at times, with shops, pubs and tenements that belong to Australia's crudest building age. And even the lofty mast of the big police radio centre, presiding over the State's 87,884 square miles and 3,113,563 people, seems like a long and bony finger admonishing those in the throbbing streets and lanes below.

But it is one of Australia's most romantic hills. It is the police hill. From here, for more than a hundred years, police history has been made.

Irish-born Peter Lalor and the goldfield rebels who fought with him against police and British troops from the crude ramparts of Ballarat's Eureka Stockade, seventy miles away, were tried not far away 111 years ago. And the still-unpublished prison governor's diaries of that age describe the thundering cheers of the freedom-loving mobs – in the court and in adjoining cells – which 'first signalled the acquittal of yet another rebel who had fought for his miner's rights.'

Ned Kelly, most famous and infamous of bushrangers, was hanged over there under the grimy dome of the old bluestone gaol now given over mainly to the rats, the pigeons, and the cooing doves above the dusty nets of spiders' webs.

Only a hundred yards away is the monument intended to remind a giddy and indifferent world of Old and New Australians that, on this hill, the eight-hour working day was born.

Leonski, the American soldier-fiend who became one of Australasia's arch-murderers, spent his last hours in the old city watch-house opposite my door before he was hanged from the same huge beam where Ned Kelly, Britain's Richard Deeming, and the woman poisoner, Martha Needle, swung.

Only ten feet from my door is the pavement beat where, in

the 1920's, 'Squizzy' (the Turk) Taylor minced up and down in bright, pointed shoes to establish bare-faced alibis in front of passing detectives whenever a gangland shooting he had ordered was about to happen miles away.

During those roaring twenties the experiments for the world's first radio car patrols were made behind these old stone walls which are the last remaining wing of the nineteenth-century Russell Street police headquarters.

I can remember some of those experiments when I was a child, and I recall standing in the bathroom of a house in Lygon Street, in the nearby Victorian-style suburb of Carlton, and being handed one ear-piece of a wireless headphone set. The man who shoved it in my hand was red-haired Senior-Constable Frederick William ('Pop') Downie, one of the enthusiastic and hard-thinking men of vision of that age who refused to accept the current convictions of American, French and British police that two-way wireless never would be effective in a car.

We listened to the faint, intriguing squeaks of Morse on a hand-made set tucked among the soap, towels and brushes on a crowded bathroom shelf. From that moment Downie, who died lamentably early when he reached inspector rank, became the 'father' of the world's present fleets of fast radio police patrols.

It was he – working with a younger disciple, Cliff Allison, who later went abroad – who convinced the sceptical police of Paris and London that the principles of primitive wireless which they understood could be applied not only to their trucks and vans. More than forty years ago he proved that wireless could and would be used in, from, and to a tourer car.

I remember that first car. It was a second-hand Palm, the first of the international flying squads. It was followed by a Hotchkiss, then by sleek Lancias and the incomparable 110 mph 'Red Streak' Daimler and its sisters, the like of which will not be seen again.

All operated from this windy hill after the State – as has been its destiny so many times – again was convulsed by passion, lust and crime.

That was Victorian Derby night, October, 1923, when one-third of the police force went on strike and anarchy overflowed as the mobs of the inlying suburbs stormed the city, murdered innocent men, derailed the trams and pillaged the shops before order was beaten and battered back to shape with the long, wooden batons of those times.

They were big cops then. Theirs was not a job for tiny men or feeble hearts.

The force, of course, had its larrikins and rogue cops. But by and large, and although they made mistakes and often had to rely on brawn as much as brains, the cops of those days were self-reliant, courageous and implacable . . . and awe-inspiring in the shiny black helmets and the grey, rustling capes with the distinctly pungent smell that was characteristic of Australian police stations at the time.

A hard world was the university of these men. They joined the force for about 6s. 6d. a day. In emergencies, which were many, they often worked four hours on and four hours off until the crisis had been met. Even at the best of times, when hours seemed more regular and reasonable, they were on duty for thirteen days on end, and in cycles that ended only once a year with a two-week break.

If single, they lived in the frigid and gloomy barracks that stood where I write. They could not marry without express permission of an aloof and haughty Chief Commissioner after the prospective bride had been 'investigated' by a senior officer.

They were almost ordered how to vote. A duty officer held a lantern in their faces at midnight to ensure that off-duty members were asleep. In the depression of the 1930's, their wages were the first to be sliced cruelly, in some cases by forty per cent.

But somehow more than a sprinkling of that old and hardy school found time and inclination to study. They remained loyal to ideals. Sometimes there were rumblings in the force. But, apart from the numbing strike, the public did not suffer.

Hearts were broken by promotion denied through prejudice, pomposity and jealousy, or the false assessment of a man. Good men were blasted by intrigue and even by a secret society that actually existed inside the force. A few are still alive to remember with bitterness.

Mark James Dooley, John Patrick Salts, Alex and Andrew McKerral, John Brophy, Frederick Piggott, Alfred George Sainsbury, Alfred Stephen Burvett, Michael Joseph Smith, Thomas John and Hugh Valentine Clugston, William Patrick Walshe, William Norman O'Mullane, James Richard (Dick) Brennan, Edmond (Ted) Ethell, and Lionel Frank Potter – these are but few of the names that come to mind when casting back to early memories and the tales of a force that took as its maxim *Tenez le droit* . . . 'Uphold what is right.'

Take Sainsbury, for instance. He rose from constable to Chief Commissioner. He wore a battered hat and, even when the State police chief, spurned the use of cars and preferred to ride to work in trams. But he won his spurs the way that dedicated police around the world are proud and happy to salute. His mission, before the First World War, was one of those true-life adventures which avid readers too often relate only to chapters on the Texas Rangers or the Royal Canadian Mounted Police.

Disguised as a hungry tramp and swagman, he trudged hundreds of miles across bush and plains in the burning heat of summer and through the freezing rains of winter. For six incredible months of hardship and loneliness he kept the faith. And he got his man – a far-north farmer, a monster in real life, who had been feeding newly-born babies to a slavering and starving sow. The farmer was a giant. Sainsbury was a small man for a policeman, and he was not armed. But he did not think of the risk he was running as he crept to the door of a barn one stormy night and, by the light of the flickering lantern inside, looked in on the devil's scene.

The quarry he had found at last had taken delivery of a babe and, with a girl moaning piteously in the straw nearby, was about to surrender it to the wild-eyed sow.

The full-throated orchestra and choir of the heavens sounded as little Sainsbury charged. He knew, through one Hogarthian hour as duty and fear nourished him to overpower the human brute and save the child, that he too would be delivered to that ravenous sow should he fail.

Consider also the late Alexander McKerral. Nothing was

beyond attempt by him. He was fine officer material – erect, sparkling-eyed, forthright and fair. For weeks back in 1918 he led packhorse teams through the treacherous mist of the jagged mountain ranges near Dargo High Plains to reach murder scenes almost as inaccessible as the legendary Shangri-La.

Back in the cities, men like these had to fight with batons and thick leather belts the bottles and boots of the bucko bands. And such were the demands made on many before the greater but easier age of science, transport and communications, that often they were forced to make decisions alone that could deter some younger men of today, and to apply, in the near-wilderness of the Australian bush, learning and knowledge that still hold the respect of the organic and inorganic scientists now inseparably associated with police work.

My father, groomed for high soldiering but apparently shaped by destiny for detective work, was one of these. He became one of the first members of 'The Terrible Ten,' a squad hand-picked to drive 'The Rileys,' 'Flying Angels,' 'Red Checker' and other bands of larrikin scum from the parks and slums of gaslit Melbourne.

But, like Downie and others, he had time for the other side of life and work. He worshipped science, although the force had no scientific laboratory. Equally he loved literature, the arts, astronomy, history and philosophy.

His friends were many and varied. He was equally pleased to chat with the late and unforgettable Major Mary Anderson, of the Salvation Army, as with the late Lieutenant-General Sir Carl Jess or the late Lieutenant-General Sir Stanley Savige; or with the playwright Louis Esson, who prowled the slums with him seeking powerful and colourful copy from a China-town of joss-houses and opium dens, of temples, and even a backyard Hindu shrine; or with James McDonald, former director of art galleries, E. J. Brady, who wrote *The Ways of Many Waters*, the late Tarlton Rayment, one of the world's renowned bee experts, the late Ralph Paull, then Chief Inspector of Pharmacies; or with the interesting muser and man of fact Charles Anthony Taylor.

Somehow my father found the time to discover and classify

the new species of bee since named after him – Halictus Dowerii – at Highett, about eight miles outside Melbourne.

And a sample of the other side of a questing policeman's life is told best by 'Jimmy' McDonald, of the National Art Gallery, in Oriel's 'Passing Show' of the *Melbourne Argus* back in 1938.

'I'll tell you a little story about a cove it's good to meet!' said Jimmy McDonald, looking down from his western window over the dusty excavations at the entrance below, where Jagger's huge artilleryman statue, in his bronze waterproof, grimly sweltered in the humidity. 'Thirty years ago I knew a policeman named Bob Dower, who used to pound a beat down by Flinders Lane, trying the locks of warehouses and always trailing thugs and thieves. Big, picturesque cove, he was. Strong as a bull. Louis Esson used to get some bright ideas for his short stories from him.

'I met Dower one night after he had arrested a gang of thieves single-handed! Knocked one out, and cracked the heads of the other two together. Just like that – all in the night's work!

'I mention this PC Dower because now he's just become Chief of the State CIB, and he's the same today as when I knew him thirty years ago. He says that circumstances helped him a lot in his promotion, but I don't know! . . . What do you think?'

During my father's term as CIB chief his fraud and larceny squad men one day told him they had checked the background of a man suspected of having stolen gold from the fabulously wealthy Golden Mile fields of Boulder, just outside Kalgoorlie in far-away Western Australia.

The smuggling of gold to India and beyond has worried Australian police at intervals for fifty years, and top security precautions are taken to protect the bullion when fortunes – as much as £150 million in gold or notes – are overlanded by desert train between Perth, Coolgardie, Kalgoorlie and Melbourne.

This man, who had been questioned during one of the periodic smuggling scares, was carrying specimens of quartz and gold which, according to earlier police information, had come from the far west and could easily point to bigger things. But, said the detectives with a distinct touch of disappointment, they had established that this man owned a mine shaft at Warrandyte, an old mining township on the upper reaches of Victoria's Yarra River. They had been up there and confirmed his claim, had checked and passed his title certificate of ownership, and been satisfied that his mine held obvious traces of gold.

It was their opinion, now, that they should free the man. He had sworn that his specimens had come legally from his mine. By all the local evidence, and despite those reports of illicit trafficking from the west, he seemed to have a genuine case and ample justification for the protests he had made.

Or was it just possible that he was putting on a clever and convincing front?

There was only one way to make sure, by a method known only to a handful, apart from scientists, at the time.

'Hold that man on some minor count,' the detectives were ordered by their chief. 'We'll have to take a calculated risk on that. Just see that, somehow, he does not leave Victoria for a day or two.'

My father's mind had darted back to years when my brother and I were kids and our east-facing kitchen every morning was lit gorgeously when the rising sun's refracted colour rays were filtered through the glass, bitumen and timber prisms he had made so often in a tiny workshop.

'I want you,' he told the wondering detectives, 'to get in touch with Melbourne University or the Royal Melbourne Institute of Technology. Get a spectroscope or have one made, and impound those samples of gold and quartz for the time being. Then come back and report.'

A specimen of this man's gold was duly lined up through a spectroscope as scientists stood by. Black lines were projected on a screen, among panels and lines of other shades.

'Now, in your expert opinion,' the neutral scientists were asked by the superintendent, 'what do those black lines mean?'

'Indisputably they reveal the presence of telluride in these specimens,' the scientists agreed.

'There is no doubt?' the superintendent pressed.

'None at all.'

'Then charge that man,' my father ordered the detectives when they had reported to him, 'with the serious theft of gold from Western Australia's Golden Mile.'

Some understandably asked why.

'Because,' my father said, 'telluride is not, and cannot be, found in any part of Victoria. This gold could not have come from Warrandyte as that man claims, or from anywhere else within two thousand miles. The Warrandyte mine was a good front. The prisoner was careful, but he lied, and he overlooked one tiny but unassailable point. His alibi is shattered (as the courts confirmed) because telluride is found in gold quartz from only one – only one – part of Australia. And that is the golden west. You ask me how I know? Because, for one thing, when I was in my teens before leaving for the South African War and enlisting in the British cavalry, I panned and dug for gold like that in those very same hot fields of Kalgoorlie's Golden Mile.'

It was 1937 before the beginnings of a scientific bureau – now a forensic science laboratory of world class – were established by Constable (later Inspector) Fred Hobley in the cold back rooms above my head. Until that year the force had been obliged to rely on its own lay resources or to call on the unusual skill of the Government pathologist, Dr Crawford Mollison, and the sagacity of Charles Anthony Taylor, 'The Cat.'

Taylor saw the early trials and errors of the police with whom he worked. Like them, his resources often were limited. But, like them, he had inexhaustible energy, profound interest in his calling, and a mind that coped best with the fresh and most complicated problems.

He was admired by the hundreds of detectives who grew grey with him, and remembered what they owed to him throughout exacting cases in the outback when a constable, or a one-stripe first-constable, commanded districts of the bush vaster than a general might direct in war.

He was equally respected by hundreds of younger men assigned in later years to 'Bonehead,' the new Detective Training College. They were astonished when they saw the specimens in his offices, first at the Health Department in fusty

Queen Street, and later at the tranquil east end of the city near Parliament House. They glimpsed crowded shelf after crowded shelf with no apparent tidiness or order. And they were equally impressed when 'The Cat,' chuckling merrily, reached into the jumble for that very bit of evidence they had suddenly demanded.

They permitted themselves a non-committal slow smile – but never a snigger or sneer – the day six bottles of beer were submitted for tests and the official answer duly was given: 'This beer is not poisoned. Two bottles are returned herewith. The other four were required for experiments.'

The range of yarns, reminiscences and predictions was almost infinite during those happy and informative years when Taylor was a frequent visitor to our home at Brighton, near the sea.

Conversation over Taylor's favourite beer, biscuits and tasty cheese ranged from diatoms and the digestive properties of fish and chips to the certainty of the atom being split one day.

Taylor struck me through those years as a kindly and disarming man with an engaging smile that contracted sharply to thin, straight and almost bloodless lips as he recited facts so clearly marshalled and so coldly clipped that there was never need for emphasis or correction, and never room for doubt.

From his boyhood days at Maryborough, then a borough in the central highlands, he had always been something of an analyst at heart. He knew the names of every wild orchid and bush flower before he was fourteen, and had closely investigated hundreds of the deep and dangerous mine shafts abandoned since the gold rush days. He once decided to become a mines expert, but discarded this idea when he graduated from the School of Mines with distinction, yet realised that the glorious age of discovery was past and that the field for exploration and research had shrunk.

He became a general teacher. He won a scholarship to the Teachers' Training College near Melbourne University. Then he plunged into a medical course. And it was here that he recognised his true bent, chemical investigation, in which he specialised.

Taylor then went back to teaching as a science master in high schools, and later was appointed to the staff of the famous Gordon Institute of Technology, at Geelong, some forty miles from Melbourne.

He worked there with Mr Jack Hennessy, in charge of the Chemical Department, and with Mr C. J. De Garis, the leader of a project known as the 'Boost Mildura and its Products Movement.'

He analysed and compared the quality and sugar content of Californian and north Victorian oranges, grapes, and other fruit – research that would be of enormous value in the investigating years to come. And he made such accurate and confident reports that he greatly helped to make the Riding of Mildura the flourishing Murray River city that it is today.

It was at the Gordon Institute that his appetite for research was whetted thoroughly, and from then on he never doubted what he would like to be.

Opportunity knocked for him in 1921 when he was selected by the Government to be Food Analyst and Deputy Chief Analyst of the Health Department under the late Mr Charles Price. A wide assortment of challenging cases soon arrived on his desk, and he plunged into them with vigour and enthusiasm that quickly marked him as an uncommon man.

When two floors of a concrete building collapsed and two men were killed, it was suspected that the concrete had not been mixed properly. But this could not be proved, the experts said, because concrete was the one thing that could not be accurately analysed. Taylor succeeded where others had failed. He pounded samples of the concrete back to dust and finally supplied the coroner's court with the exact proportions of the imperfect mix.

When Arnold Karl Sodeman, a fiendish child slayer, was arrested for the murder of a little girl, he boastfully admitted having also killed three other girls. Most top police on the job energetically discounted this confession. But, as will be seen later, the uncanny Taylor dug into records made twenty years earlier. Again he won over and amazed even the most cynical unbelievers by proving that Sodeman was telling the truth.

In 1935 the badly burned body of an Italian was found beyond the north-east suburb of Balwyn, in a culvert. Police and pathologists could not determine the exact cause of death, but thought he may have been battered brutally. Inevitably, Taylor was called in on the case, and soon he told an astonished audience they had a rare case of two-stroke murder.

He was not content with only the evidence on the spot. He insisted on seeing the room where the man had lived, and was taken to a small bedroom above a fruit shop in Richmond, on the perimeter of Melbourne city. Taylor became engrossed in scores of tiny brown spots on a wall beside the bed, pinpoint spots so fine that they had not aroused attention.

He insisted they were microscopic spots of blood. The pathologists agreed – after Taylor had prised some spots off the wall and given them the chemical and filter paper reaction test that produced a deep and unmistakable blue. But no one could suggest how the spots had flown there so finely until the analyst's reconstruction again proved him correct. He claimed that the Italian had not been killed and set on fire at the culvert. He had been murdered in this room, and the causes of death were twofold.

He insisted that the Italian had first been battered savagely, possibly to death, certainly towards the dangerous point of death. Then he had been strangled. But, said Taylor, at some stage of the strangling operation the grip on the victim's throat had been relaxed for a split second. The air in the lungs had expanded then, and caused the blood in the throat to spray like mist. The murderer broke down when this precise reconstruction was put to him.

A grotesque legs and arms mystery of the thirties has never been solved. But Taylor's work on it was quickly completed and should still be on record somewhere to prove again, if ever an arrest is made, that once more he was right. After the limbs had been fished from the Yarra River, near Melbourne, pathologists and police were unable to decide whether they had been severed from a male or female trunk. The size of the hands and feet suggested they were female. But this was not conclusive. They could just as easily have been a boy's.

Taylor spent hours examining the under side of the fingernails through a microscope and scraped out the last unwashed deposit of dirt that probably was invisible to even the sharpest naked eyes.

The deduction he drew was that the limbs were those of a woman domestic who probably scoured with sandsoap and wore a blue dress while she was lighting fires and cleaning grates.

Only when the spotlight of an outraged law was shining brightly did this little-known expert who was a legend among all who worked with him suddenly leave the wings and become the star player in so many of Australia's bush and city dramas. When the show was over he would return to near-obscurity, to his cloistered offices and their atmosphere rich with chemical odours, doubtful butter, sealed bottles, soldered tins, retorts, test-tubes and all the other apparatus of a craft that could even tell him that two small fish he once found in a tin of sardines were more than twenty years old.

'I was fated to find my way into medico-legal work and nature was kind enough to fit me for it temperamentally,' he recalls. 'It was inevitable as the destiny of a piece of steel snapped up by a magnet.

'In 1901 Australia was experiencing a particularly severe drought. Unemployment was rife and, as a youngster of fifteen, I realised I had to find work in some form. My own ideas of life had been coloured by my boyhood in Maryborough, a country township which looked back hungrily to those prosperous gold rush days half a century before. I was at a loose end. I had no idea what my own tendencies were, though I suppose I should have guessed that I had a submerged hankering to probe with scientific things. As a kid, I had wandered round the bush studying flowers with an analytical eye. I knew the name, shape and characteristic of every orchid and I was intrigued by their colouring and growth. I used to explore old mine shafts, wanting to know every why and wherefore of them. Mining first attracted me. After leaving secondary school, I went on to the School of Mines. Perhaps I was not quite satisfied. Anyway, I allowed an aunt, herself a teacher, to induce me to fill a vacancy on the staff of a Maryborough school. Then I was chosen to open a new school at Avoca, in the north. It was charming bushland country where magnificent walnut trees, planted soon after the dawn of Australia's civilised history, grew close to the utter desolation left by the alluvial gold rush. But I was restless. A thirst for knowledge almost overpowered me. Diligence brought me two years' free studentship at the Melbourne Teachers' Training College – the guerdon of competitive examination. Science was my choice. It was exacting, but I liked its rigid standard of efficiency and the insistent appeal of its biological and chemical aspects. Almost before I knew it, I had launched myself into a medical course. But later I did not adopt medicine for a career because I analysed myself and realised that my temperament was really not in tune with a doctor's life. Then I found the opening I had been longing for – science associated with our primary products, and the study of these at Colac, Warragul, Benalla, Daylesford, Geelong, and other parts of our rolling countryside. This idea appealed to me. It was Australia rising from the ashes left by the great gold fever. My big chance came when I was appointed to the staff of the Gordon Institute of Technology at Geelong. I learned a lot. I dreamed some golden dreams. But since that moment, which led to my appointment first as Deputy Government Analyst for the Crown, I never doubted what I wanted to be.'

Several witnesses remain to testify that he chose well. Among them is Victoria's Crown Solicitor, Mr Tom Mornane, who remembers Taylor as 'an extraordinary man.'

A ready tribute also comes from Dr Norman McCallum, Ph.D., M.Sc., who, as director of the Victoria Police forensic laboratory, is Taylor's successor of more modern times.

McCallum, also well-known at Scotland Yard, Harvard University, and in Pittsburgh and other theatres, declares that Taylor was 'unique.'

'Charlie had to do the lot alone – all branches of science and toxicology which, these days, are handled in separate and almost independent bureaus,' Dr McCallum says. 'He mastered every branch. He is the last and best of a vanished race.'

Another admirer is Mr Pat Shea, who retired in 1963 as surveyor to the Office of Titles of the Crown Law Department.

'Back in the thirties I had the honour to be classified as one of "The Big Four" called in early on every important murder probe,' he says. 'The others were "The Cat," the Government pathologist, the late Dr Crawford Mollison, and Fred Hobley, who established the police scientific bureau and photographic sections as a young constable and rose to command them as an inspector. Taylor was an exceptional man. Academically he was outstanding, and his practical application of knowledge was always surprising. He was very determined, too – as those who crossed his path found out – because he was never defeated in the courts. And so I say that, outside his vast knowledge, one of his greatest assets was an almost pugnacious resolution never to be beaten by the other man.'

Mr Taylor lived to be eighty. His health failed and he became frail. He was retired several years and lived quietly in a cosy but unpretentious red-brick villa in Cole Street, Gardenvale, near the bayside just south-east of Melbourne.

It is unfortunate that age and illness prevented every one of Taylor's triumphs being fully told. I should, for example, like to recall in detail the Kinglake murder of the wooltruck driver, John Thomas Demsey, back in 1938. It was one of the rare major crimes recorded on Australia's best-known sporting day, Melbourne Cup Day. There were three early cardinal features in this crime. A hijacked truck with a valuable wool cargo was found in forest so dense and dangerous that a low-flying reconnaissance aircraft was hired by police from the RAAF for the first time. The second point was that the driver's body, in a shallow bush grave under a mantle of bracken and bark, was stumbled on days later some distance from the abandoned truck. But the components of the third feature remained baffling. Where and when was this driver killed? And exactly what route and through what time span could the truck have passed – driven by Demsey or his assassins? – after it was last seen scores of miles away, and days earlier, on a country highway?

Taylor was the one who came up with the answers. He made a careful study of the rainfall charts, varying earth and mud, and the partly digested contents of the dead man's stomach. He drew a tiny circle on a map and said: 'Inside here was the last known spot where the man could have been alive and well. But he also died within the perimeter of this circle.'

Then he gave the approximate time of death, within an hour as the backtrack later proved, and accurately drew the line the truck had been driven by the killers.

Unhappily, the engaging and absorbing backgrounds to such crime stories often do not find a place in durable but dull official police records. Their spice is savoured by one man, or by someone who knows him. In the case of Taylor, I probably know more about the handling of his cases than anyone else. He was never known to brag. In fact, he rarely talked about his work. His disclosures to me were made possible largely through family associations which he respected.

Taylor appears in every story in this selection, from sabotage and multiple murder to near-folksy but unfortunate anecdotes of the simple hearth. Sometimes the story is a vehicle to carry Taylor's work. Sometimes Taylor is both rider and mount. But all cases chronicle a long and interesting era of medico-legal history which otherwise might not be told, for it bares secrets of several famous cases and discloses others for the first time.

Those who have shared these secrets many years have helped me because none dispute that Taylor's work in these and other cases rank him as a criminologist of world class.

It has been my fortune to know many of that class. I admire 'Wee Willie' Merrilees, Scotland's 'pocket battleship' – the tough but perceptive chief constable of the Lothians and Peebles Constabulary, who can feel dried perspiration on his steering wheel and decide who last drove his car without permission. He is the shortest, and probably the most extraordinary, policeman I have met.

The late Superintendent Wilf Daws of Scotland Yard, who hunted the swashbuckling smuggler-murderer and suicide Ronald Chesney, was one of the most tenacious and implacable manhunters of his time.

Commissaire Edmund Sebeille, of the Marseilles Brigade Mobile, revealed the same unrelenting, but almost inhuman and humourless doggedness when he cracked the murders of Sir Jack and Lady Drummond and their daughter Elizabeth, in the peaceful south of France.

I have met brilliant scientists and G-men of the FBI's outstanding and dedicated leader, J. Edgar Hoover, a man with illuminated pages in my book of praise.

Signor Giuseppe Dosi, former Chief Commissioner of Police in Rome, was equally convincing disguised as an Arabian or a Bolshevist, or when silently co-operating with Americans to cancel 'Lucky' Luciano's passport and exile him in South Italy until his death.

I found the late Dr Harry Soderman, Swedish scientist for Interpol and UNO, to be the adventurously scientific mind behind many police chiefs of the world.

The late Sir Bernard Spilsbury has never been forgotten by Victoria's former Chief Commissioner, Mr Alex Duncan, and others who worked with both of them from Scotland Yard.

Sir Joseph Simpson and Sir Richard Jackson of the Yard, Marcel Sicot and Jean Nepote of Paris's Interpol headquarters, Florent Louwage of Belgium, Herr Paul Dickopf and Herr Wolfram Sangmeister of West Germany – these are among others who have helped me to recognise and evaluate the talents and gifts required for fighting and detecting crime.

Yet Taylor remains in a class apart.

Energetic but scholarly, tenacious yet patient, and equipped with encyclopaedic knowledge and the brain to deploy it, he accepted challenges during years when science, fingerprinting, photography and other techniques awed and dazzled many of the rising generation, and were almost spurned by the stolid champions of the older school.

Although he does not claim it, he left a legacy that many investigators today could profitably try to imitate. In a more scientific than technical sense, his faith, outlook and approach resembled those of Dr Hans Gross, Professor of Criminology at Prague University in the last century, who gave world police their first practical manual of instruction in his *System der Kriminalistik* or *Criminal Investigation*.

The tribute paid to Gross could apply equally to Taylor in his field: 'an indefatigable observer; a far-seeing psychologist, full of ardour to unearth the truth . . . a clever craftsman; in turn draughtsman, photographer, modeller, armourer . . . he opens to us the researches and experiences of many years.'

Taylor's message of concentrated reasoning, which he gives here, is one that any dedicated law officer should not forget.

He broke away from accepted dogma and conformity and found ample room for exercising a healthy, independent mind. He volunteered the warning that 'there may be several among his calling now who criticise his technique and approach.' But we are reminded that 'the history of medicine was written in blood-red words by the individuals who forsook the safe but dull world of convention.'

For years at Australian police headquarters I have asked this question of others who knew him well – the Arnolds, Duncans, Pettys, Wilbys, Jacksons, Rosengrens, Donellys, Craigs, Adams, Piggotts, Matthews, McMennemins, Davidsons, Hollands, Sakers and McCallums: 'How did this man, Taylor, rate with you?' And the answer always was: 'A shrewd and clever thinker, patient and exact, an unflinching witness, and an undefeated one.'

These selections from war and peace should tell the reader why. Then one may wonder how a community could have sent such a distinguished servant into obscurity without just reward.

Perhaps it is a colonial relic that has lingered long enough. Whatever the reason, Taylor was prepared to shrug it off with just an echo of the traditional warning put to prisoners when at last they have decided to confess: 'After being made aware of my rights, without fear of punishment or hope of reward, I make the following statement. . . .'

Charles Anthony Taylor lived for one week past his eightieth birthday, long enough to set his seal of approval on this account of his life and work and to provide a personal foreword for it.

His body was cremated at Springvale, some fourteen miles from Melbourne.

Two months later 'The Cat's' friend and firm admirer, Alex Duncan, died. It was as though, in the late summer of 1965, an era was passing.

A.D.

Russell Street Police Headquarters,
Melbourne, Australia.

1 Hanged by Human Hairs

TAYLOR has never forgotten nor regretted the early and uneasy chapters of his Crown career when medico-legal science was spurned by many as a new-fangled plaything, and treated mainly with suspicion and rarely with respect. So it is understandable that he remembered vividly the memorable murder trial of Colin Ross. Not only was it said to be the first time that medico-legal science of this kind was used to provide evidence in Australasian courts. It also marked its admission as an indispensable ally of criminal investigation and prosecution.

The fate of Colin Ross, a hang-dog fellow accused of murdering little Alma Tirtschke with the lovely hair, seemed very much in doubt during the early days of the trial. Ross had quite stout alibis, including one provided by his girl friend, Gladys Wain, who had been in his shady wine saloon at the time he was alleged to have murdered Alma there.

Police and counsel clashed for hours when the trial argument reached a bitter level in February, 1922, and the court was electrified as suddenly Ross screamed that he had been framed by police. His blind and brilliant lawyer, Maxwell, rose and bowed. He was hurt and deeply moved, and asked to be 'disassociated from his client's outburst' because there had been no suggestion of a frame-up until this critical moment in the trial.

That was when every doubt and argument in Ross's favour seemed to be smashed beyond repair by a few strands of human hair and the sturdy confidence of two Australian scientists, who agreed that those few gleaming strands should be strong enough to hang a man.

The men were the then Government Analyst, Mr Charles Price, and his up and coming deputy of thirty-six, Charles Taylor.

When Melbourne – and all Australia, for that matter – was stirred by this Gun Alley murder, it was a gracious and fast-changing city passing through a rugged and colourful era. It was basking in the peace following the First World War, jealous of its own Dame Nellie Melba and its acknowledged leadership in Australian culture, the theatre and the arts.

But at the Bourke Street Strand Theatre one could see *Those American Boys* flickering for sixpence. Mary Miles Minter was showing at the Majestic. 'Fatty' Arbuckle was in *The Desert Hero* at the Auditorium, and at the Tivoli, Hugh D. McIntosh's *Oddments* was received by press critics with 'uproarious laughter and unlimited approval.'

Satin shoes were selling for 6s. 6d. a pair, and button boots for 12s. 6d.

Everyone was breezily blowing bubbles, Mary Lou had made a musical debut, Georgia was on every bobbed, shingled and cloche-hatted mind, and nothing could be finer than to be in Carolina, even if no one had bananas and the rose still grew in No Man's Land.

Down at Allan's music store the song hits of the time, two shillings a score, were *Everything Is Peaches* and *That Old-fashioned Mother of Mine.*

It was an age of beauty and brass, of baroque and bawdy houses; of bodkins and beads; of bowlers and the Royal Navy's mighty battleships; of beatitudes or booze and bedlam; of courtliness and charm; and of thick soup strained through the last of the Kitchener Moustaches.

But Melbourne had another world beyond the gridiron tracks of the clanging cable trams. The queen city of the south, the moneybags of Australia, was a lady of gay and quality crinolines and long skirts with dirty linen underneath.

Saloons for snooker, two-up and grog-and-knuckle fights flourished on Sunday mornings behind a haze of sweat, vomit, alcohol and eucalyptus fumes. The pointed shoes of Squizzy (the Turk) Taylor already were as synonymous with evil as would be the fur-trimmed coat of Al Capone in America in a few years' time. The dim streets of Collingwood, Carlton, Fitzroy and other inlying suburbs were fearsome arenas for nightly battles between the brawny, black-helmeted police and the pariahs who found strength and comfort with their roaming gangs. And the heart of the city unashamedly condoned narrow, squalid Little Lonsdale Street, the hub of the dangerous and dreadful slums, the ghastly 'red light mile' of pimps, prowlers, gunmen and two hundred known prostitutes who beckoned from the worn bluestone steps of reeking dens.

The city and the dark suburbs hugging it depended on the system of one big beat constable to every city square, while the era saw the last phase of the almost time-honoured 'sugar bag' system. This was the full pint of foaming beer left at the back lane doors of many pubs after dark for some of the thirsty patrolling gendarmes to have with their wives' cheese and beef sandwiches.

The force was only two years from the mutinous strike by six hundred police that would allow unbridled lawlessness to rule Melbourne for a week. But until then it was governed with a baton of iron wielded by the Chief Commissioner's office behind the Gothic front of the City Court.

On the bluestone wall of the police headquarters wing, which still stands, a large brass plate proclaimed that the CIB really was the Detective Force. It was proud, sometimes imperious, and often vain. Occasionally it was insular and arrogant. Almost disdainfully and near-defiantly it detached itself from the main body of the force. It was even patronisingly tolerant of its own plain-clothes branch of mature yet junior satellites and 'apprentices.' Graciously it surrendered to these sterling men the inquiries that involved property worth less than £50. Jealously it reserved the monopoly to give its unctuous blessing and efforts to investigations above that mark.

Potter was a big and respected name in this detective force. It had been from the moment he dedicated himself to forming Australia's first fingerprint bureau. Harold and Leslie Saker, Ted Ethell, Ernest Ashton, Daniel Mulfahey, Dick Brennan and many others were spoken of as proven men or promising young colts. And of the feared sub-officers in the field none surrounded himself with greater awe than slim, dapper Frederick Piggott and heavy-jowled, beetle-browed John Brophy, whose later fall from grace – after being shot at night – caused the scandal that led to the Royal Commission on the force and the resignation of its chief, Major-General (later Field Marshal) Sir Thomas Blamey.

The guys and dolls raised their bottles and chipped glasses in the flophouses of those days, fatalistically agreeing that:

'Ashes to ashes, and dust to dust;
If Brophy doesn't get you, Piggott must.'

Bourke Street was a honky-tonk avenue of spruikers, streamers, theatres and cinemas that still showed the silent flicks. It backed on to rows of market stalls and sideshows known as the Eastern Market and the Eastern Arcades. The whole was a vast, bizarre, enthralling network of stone arcades and lofty corridors and unexpected corners where men went to buy their fodder, tools and harness, ancient books or bargain clothes. One went there to be tattooed, to consult phrenologists, to gulp cheap slugs of muscat, port or sherry, or have one's uncertain fortune told in the crystal ball of 'The Russian Seer, Madame Gurkha.'

There were caves of draughts and odours, of dust hovering along shafts of filtered light. Here was the retreat for derelicts, the meeting-place for the knockabout men of town, and the heaven of the kids.

Alma Tirtschke, thirteen, was one of the merry thousands of her age, with stardust in her eyes, who could not resist the tarnished charm and glitter of the great arcades. It was their fantasyland in the Melbourne of the period. She came skipping and lilting there on the summer afternoon of December 30, 1921, a gay little schoolgirl wearing a serge uniform that highlighted the red tint of her hair. It was hair that soon would make her one of the most talked-about schoolgirls in the world.

There may have been no story, and Ross may have gone free, or never rated a reputation heavier than a petty thug's, if some other child with black, yellow, or nondescript hair had passed this way that day.

The morning of December 31, 1921, was warm in Melbourne. It was New Year's Eve. Alma's body was found on the cobbles off Gun Alley, a lane opposite the arcade's south arches, facing Little Collins Street. This alley disappeared when car showrooms were built over it. It was only about fifty yards east of the present Pink Alley, which was its twin and ran north to south.

Very few of the notables called in on this famous case are alive today. Frederick Piggott, who retired as a senior superintendent in 1938, died at the north Victorian city of Mildura in 1962, at the age of eighty-four. Brophy, too, is dead. The youngest, debonair Harold Saker, one of the well-known police family, has retired after years as chief stipendiary steward of country racing clubs.

Not long before he died I talked again with Piggott at his home, and poured over neat files kept for almost sixty years. I said to him: 'Outlines of the death of Alma Tirtschke and the trial of Colin Ross have been written many times. But the background stories are still not known. Mr Taylor will tell us for the first time exactly how the hairs were found. Would you concentrate on the police points which convince you still, apart from the medico-legal evidence, that Ross was guilty of the crime? I ask this because, even today, there are people who still believe Ross's protests that the girl in his 'plonk' saloon that night was not Alma Tirtschke.

'As I have always understood it, such doubts rested mainly on allegations that much of the trial evidence against Ross, apart from the scientific evidence, came from criminals and declared prostitutes who were anxious to share in the £1,000 reward offered for information leading to the conviction of the murderer. Others, I understand, were not satisfied by the testimony of Ivy Matthews, described at the time as a "mystery woman" who refused to give the court past details of her life. These do not claim that Ross was innocent. But some, like Hugh Buggy, a perceptive crime reporter of that time, do deeply question much of the evidence of Ivy Matthews, the Crown's chief lay witness. And they are inclined to repudiate her repeated avowals of respectability.'

In his prime Piggott was a lean, well-dressed figure who

twirled a cane, elegantly flicked ash from long cigars, and set his homburg or bowler at a rakish tilt. He was hawk-nosed, had sensitive lips and shrewd eyes that narrowed so often he had developed at their corners those crow's-feet characteristics of Australian outbackers who squint across shimmering plains.

He drew his dressing-gown together, and said: 'There was a lot of bitterness about the case. I had not intended to open old sores and wounds. But because there is no doubt in my mind that Ross was the guilty man, I will release some facts not known even to the jury when Ross was tried. On the morning of New Year's Eve, 1921, the chief of detectives, Superintendent Lionel Frank Potter, came to our old muster room at Russell Street headquarters and told me to go down with Brophy to the city morgue in Batman Avenue. He said a girl's body had been taken there and that he felt it would be a complicated case.

'I said to Potter: "But if this girl's body was found in the city, that's Brophy's division, the city division area. I'm on the south of the city division."

' "I know that," he said. "But you also happen to be the senior man. I'll need you both on this case. I'm emphasising that already I feel this will be a complicated case. So let me know, soon, what you think about the body."

'Almost as soon as I saw it I was certain that it had been washed after death. If true, that was most unusual. And the reason was no clearer when the Government pathologist, Dr Crawford Mollison, came in and certified that the girl had been strangled and washed and dried after death.

'A "bottle-o" had found the body about 6 a.m. that day. It was naked and lying face upwards on cobbles, with the shiny hair splayed out backwards. Two deductions appeared to be justified. First, that her body had been carried to the spot at night and that her hair had splayed out when something underneath – a blanket or sack perhaps – had then been tugged out from under her.

'Second, she had been killed at a point not far distant. It was inconceivable, even in those dimly-lit days, that she could have been carried a long way. Cars were not as common in

Melbourne then, and it was unlikely that anyone would have clattered over the cobbles with one of the many ironshod horse carts or buggies of those times.

'Dr Mollison had told us the girl had been dead about eight hours when her body was found. Therefore, the killer had more than twelve hours' start on us, ample time to destroy vital evidence and start fabricating a reasonable alibi.

'But until now the world does not know how or why the killer got that start, which allowed him to tear up clothes and blankets, to wash out his wine saloon and clean the body, and then to compose himself. He got that advantage through the failure of a uniformed constable to do his duty properly on that one night of the year.

'It came about this way. The crime has always been known as the Gun Alley Murder. But the body was not quite in Gun Alley. Gun Alley, like nearby Pink Alley today, ran north and south. Near its south end, a five-foot wide squalid lane, crowded with dustbins or trash cans, ran off towards the east like the top arm of a reversed and inverted L. This arm was a short, blind cul-de-sac, and just about where it branched off at right angles from the end of Gun Alley the iron grille of a drain was let into the cobbles. Nearby was an old street-lamp, good enough to show anyone passing along Little Collins Street whether someone was lurking up Gun Alley.

'In a way, it's probably a pity it was shining at all that night.

'Now, Alma was killed about 9 p.m. But her naked body must have been dumped in that cul-de-sac off the alley some time after 1 a.m. We were convinced of that because we knew a prostitute who had been at the spot just before one. Her information had always been utterly reliable, and she swore there was no sign of the body or a prowler at that time.

'Probably less than an hour after that prostitute left the cul-de-sac a beat constable came down Little Collins Street. It was his duty to check every lane and alley on his block. We did not doubt that he peered into the approaches of Gun Alley with his torch, and saw the lighted lamp at the south end. He was right enough in assuming that there was nothing in Gun Alley itself to warrant his attention, but because of this he just did not bother to walk only a few more yards up the alley and glance into the cul-de-sac leading to the left. Although I'm now an old man and forty years have passed since then, I still get angry when I think of it. If that constable had only done his routine duty properly, he could not have missed seeing Alma's body just round the corner.

'We were satisfied the body was dumped there between the time the prostitute left the lane and when this constable arrived nearby. And we realised later that the killer – Ross – was actually kneeling or standing beside the naked body with his heart in his throat while the constable was walking just a few yards away!

'That accounts for our conviction that Ross originally did not intend to have Alma's body found, but panicked and fled after trying to push it down the grille into the drain. Had he been seen there would have been no tiring backtrack for us and no far-and-wide search for those little bits of necessary evidence. And, of course, there would have been no sensational case for young Charles Anthony Taylor to cut his court-room teeth on.

'But as it was, Jack Brophy and I spent the next few days and nights checking every one of the strange types who frequented the arcades nearby. We eliminated hundreds. Naturally, we soon had Ross and others like him in our sights, but we had an open mind. We knew Ross had kept a low-class wine saloon that was a hideout for thieves, thugs and prostitutes. But there were many equally unsavoury types in that quarter. For example, there was a group of three including a daily newspaperman who were belting up a really hot life in a room of the arcade and hoping to keep it dark. Jointly or individually, I suppose, they could have had many strange impulses towards a sexual crime. But they were still only possibilities in our minds.

'My own suspicions did not harden until one afternoon when Brophy and I were strolling down Little Collins Street from the east end. I saw this Ross ahead of us and I said to Brophy: "Jack, I think I'll push on and have a yarn with that Ross fellow."

'Jack agreed we had better check him. "He's not much

chop," he said. "The licence of that rotten plonk shop of his expired on New Year's Eve. He was being forced to close the very day of the murder. He must have been hanging around the night before." '

Piggott agreed. But he believes he betrayed no feelings of suspicion as he hurried to face Ross under the lofty wrought-iron arch of the arcade.

'Ah, good afternoon, Mr Ross,' he greeted the other breezily. 'You remember me, of course? Yes, we have met before. Piggott, from the Detective Office. We talked the other day about this little girl. Shocking case, Mr Ross. Brutally outraged. But I'd like to find out if she came here on her own that day.'

Ferret-faced Ross was eager to help. 'Oh, yes, Mr Piggott,' he volunteered quickly. 'I saw her here alone.'

Words came tumbling from him as Piggott listened shewdly and nodded approval.

'She was wearing a pleated skirt, a white blouse, a white hat with a red band, and boots or shoes – boots, I think. Pretty kid, she was. Shining red-gold hair hanging down her back . . .'

Bells were ringing in Piggott's head as Ross added trivial details of the girl's appearance that had not been published in the press.

'When Ross was on the gallows trap later, he swore by Almighty God that he had never seen Alma Tirtschke,' Piggott told me as he continued. 'Yet that afternoon he not only declared he had seen her, but gave me an accurate description of her. I had tried to be as casual as possible. Ross was bending over backwards to be co-operative, outwardly shocked by a callous murder. But it was throbbing in my head – how could any man remember such a description of a passing schoolgirl if he had seen her only briefly in a milling crowd and had no special reason to remember her? I continued our conversation on a general note, and then I pointed my cigarette towards one of the shopfronts inside the arcade near Ross's closed-down saloon. It was the nightly bolt-hole of the newspaperman and his friends.

' "Who's over there, Mr Ross?" I asked. "What's the strength of that place?"

'Ross revealed his twin rows of gold and metal teeth and leered. "Ah, now you're talking," he said. "They're a queer crowd over there. Often take in little tarts. Ha! I think you're on the right track now."

'I didn't press him. Nor did I inform him that we already had checked the three who went to the shop. We had a pretty fair idea what they were up to. Homosexuality with all sorts of twists. But we were reasonably confident it didn't include murder.

'I went back to Brophy and said: "Well, Jack, it seems to me it could be this Ross fellow." But we had no witnesses. We had not even found the girl's clothes. Hundreds of crackpots were trying to confuse us by consistently scattering buttons and other articles near the scene of the crime and claiming they had belonged to Alma.

'Even at this stage we had a presentiment that there would be a terrific battle at the trial as lawyers attacked the evidence we presented, including that of Ivy Matthews and some gaol-birds – those whom Ross's blind barrister, Maxwell, later was to dub scathingly "the quintet of reputables and disreputables." But our first break came when scattered shreds of dark serge material were found near the Footscray Road, three or four miles from the city. They were identified as pieces of Alma's missing uniform, and they had been found in the direction of Ross's home.

'It wasn't a bad start. It pointed nowhere near a conviction, let alone a watertight case. But we thought it promising enough to concentrate on Ross.

'Another break came up when we met "The Man With The Staring Eyes." He was first to tell us of strange movements near the arcade on the night of the murder. Others came up with similar versions later, but "Staring Eyes" was the first to put us on this tack. The world had not heard of him before because the few of us who met him had never seen him before that day and have never seen or heard of him again. But you have my word that he did exist.

'Before he vanished he swore that the night Alma was murdered he saw Ross in Little Collins Street near the Eastern Arcade. Well after midnight, he claimed, he watched Ross creep from his saloon to the arch of the arcade and glance furtively up and down the gloomy street. Apparently Ross could not see anyone and quickly disappeared. But "Staring Eyes" waited. He was one of those knockabout types who could see through men like Ross, and he knew he was up to no good.

'Sure enough, Ross appeared again at the arcade entrance. It was then after 1 a.m. Ross was carrying something upright and struggled with it across Little Collins Street towards Gun Alley. "Staring Eyes" was some distance away and did not want to be seen. He did not move into the street or go near the alley because, for his own reasons, he did not want to be seen by the constable who was due soon to pass down the street. But he had seen enough to confirm our suspicion that Alma's body had been carried to the dumping spot "standing up."

'Unfortunately, this evidence was not produced at the coroner's court, nor at the trial, because our man with the staring eyes had melted into thin air. But gradually, and by hard slogging, we built up a hardening case against Ross, enough to warrant raiding his house out at Footscray.

'With young Detective Harold Saker, Brophy, Ashton and others, we vaulted back fences and took Ross by surprise. In one of his rooms we found blankets and strips of blanket which, it was fair to surmise, could have been used to enshroud Alma's body when it was lugged from the saloon to the cul-de-sac. We were certain she had been covered that night. "Staring Eyes" had spoken of "an irregularly shaped bundle or person in Ross's arms." It was inconceivable to us that a killer would have tried to move a female body through even dimly-lit streets without covering it. We were also doubtful that a hessian bag had been used, although Ross had many for his horse, because, taking the washing of the body into account, there was not a trace of fibre on the body or in the hair.

'We took statements from several persons who had been patrons of Ross's sloppy wine saloon. Ross had had his little private parlour behind the gaudy and clinking bead curtains fashionable in those days. Whenever the beads were parted the customers could see some of the parlour contents. Among these, they told us, were blankets similar to those we seized at Footscray. An interesting point was that there were no such blankets in the parlour when it was searched by police.

'I believe they had been removed to Ross's home, almost certainly the night Alma died. But that seemed difficult to prove. Remember, Alma's body had been washed carefully. And our inquiries revealed that, during that New Year's Eve morning or the night before, Ross had thoroughly washed out his parlour.

'Now that was hardly consistent with a man who had never bothered about hygiene and was suffering from venereal disease. But the actions *were* consistent with those of a guilty man determined to remove damning stains such as blood, vomit, liquor or hairs and fibres from his surroundings and the flesh of a victim who had been there.

'By this time, the public were clamouring for police action and the politicians, of course, were harassing us. They were nervy, thankless days. But we survived the uproar long enough to plump for the theory that Ross ravished and strangled Alma in the saloon, washed the body to remove all stains, wrapped it in one or more blankets, dumped the body after trying to force it down a grille, whisked the blankets from under her, hid them at home, returned to the saloon and washed it, and went home again.

'In those colourful but tough times a policeman was expected to be a near-genius during any crisis. But we were well aware that our evidence to back our reasoning was only circumstantial at this stage. We thought it was really very good. We were sure we had our man. But we still had to hope that, by hard slogging, we would get even more positive evidence that would stick hard in court and break Ross down.

'Harold Saker borrowed a dray and harnessed up one of the trooper's horses from the police depot. This combination was similar to one Ross had often used between his saloon and home. Saker covered the distance several times. Sometimes he used alternative means, including buses, trams, trains and a bicycle. But one part of his route was common to all – the part of the Footscray Road where the scraps of Alma's uniform had been found.

'Saker soon convinced us that Ross – if he claimed in defence that he was home during those vital hours early in New Year's Eve – could have accomplished everything we were going to allege, and also have time to go home twice.

'We arrested Ross and charged him with murder. At the inquest he was committed for trial.

'We realised, however, that time was running out. But whether for Ross or us we really were not sure. The days ahead were precious. It was a time for us to stay cool and keep our heads as a wave of crazy emotion swept Melbourne. Charlie Taylor can prove how calm we had to be. I can return to my part of the story when he's revealed what went on in his laboratory with Mr Price.'

* * *

On the stroke of ten on January 13, 1922, the day after Ross was arrested, Senior-Detective Frederick Piggott carefully knocked the ash from a long cigar and strode into the Government Analyst's bureau of the Health Department in Queen Street, Melbourne. Thankfully he dumped a bulky brown paper parcel on a table. He was inscrutable as usual as he untied the bindings, withdrew three blankets, and laid them out before Price and Taylor.

'Now,' he began, blowing neat rings of smoke, 'we are hoping that these may help to put friend Ross on ice. What way is there to get proof that, although they were found at his house, one or more of these blankets came from Ross's wine saloon, and had come in contact with the body of Alma Tirtschke after it had been washed?'

None in the laboratory that hot morning knew that, during the following two weeks, the scientists would resort to methods that would make a few weightless hairs lower those delicately balanced scales of justice.

In the magnificent crime laboratory of the FBI in Washington not long ago I was intrigued by the gigantic model of a human hair mounted on a wall above the microscopes and spectrographs of the bureau's many scientists. Probably it is eighteen feet long and two feet thick, the size of a sturdy Australian bluegum. It may be ten million times the size of a human hair, and its network of black and red lines accurately traces the whole physical structure of a hair like a road map or complex underground railway system. It is admirable proof of the stride taken by science since 1922, when Price and Taylor began their own research into the characteristics, structure and varieties of human hair.

In one corner of the Melbourne laboratory was a plywood screen painted white. Over this Taylor draped the first blanket.

'For about an hour,' he told me, 'I scanned the first blanket inch by inch, peering at it through a good hand lens never more than about six inches off. I told Price I had drawn a blank. On that blanket was not one visible stain, tear, cigarette burn, fibre, or unusual speck of powder, glass, mucous, charcoal or sawdust.'

But the second blanket soon focused his rapt attention. In the top left corner was a hair. It appeared to be a human hair of a striking and uncommon shade. By mid-afternoon, twenty-two hairs of different lengths had been found. None was disturbed. The position of each was marked carefully with a safety pin.

'Good work,' said Piggott. 'But whose hairs are they?'

'We must be cautious here,' Taylor warned gently. 'I did not say they were human hairs. I said they seem to be. This sort of work is new and tricky. We have now to try to establish if they are the girl's.'

Taylor mounted each hair on a four-by-two-inch strip of white cardboard, fastening them with Canadian balsam, an adhesive used then for mounting microscope slides. Each was covered with a window of transparent tape so that handling would not injure them.

Hairs from several of Alma Tirtschke's head were also mounted on similar slides.

'My first observation was that some of the hairs found on the blanket were shorter than others,' Taylor said as he broke the silence of forty years. 'Some were only four to five inches long. Others were up to twelve inches long. We were not living when the present long-haired cult was fashionable. Therefore, the defence could hardly argue that these long hairs had come from a male head. On the other hand, could counsel insist that the short ones had, and had probably belonged to one of Ross's men friends? In my opinion this theory would never be supported because, in every case, the short hairs were broken. Not one had the bulb that can be found at the root of a full hair.

'But every unbroken hair was longer than a man's. And each of these did have a bulb. So my first conclusion was that the hairs definitely had come from a female head. It was also obvious to us that the hairs had one point in common. They were coarse, quite unusually coarse, but equally and evenly coarse. The microscope proved that. We compared the hairs from the blanket with those taken from Alma's head and found that these specimens were identically coarse.

'Our next step was some analysis of pigmentation. Coloration comes into hair when a person is about six years old. It reaches its peak about seven or eight years later – about Alma's age – and usually it stays that way for several years. Between the ages of thirty and fifty, the pigmentation often begins to decline. At this stage people say they are going grey. But that is not so. There is no such thing as a strictly grey hair.

'Hairs are either pigmented or white. Greyness is almost an illusion. It is a blend of coloured hairs and white ones. Even boys born with snowy hair do not have strictly white hairs. Their hairs are creamy and have some pigmentation.

'Back in 1922 I knew that our gathering knowledge of these and other facts about hair could be vital either way in the Colin Ross case because we were treading very carefully with medico-legal opinion then. On the Crown side, we believed that all the hairs found on the blanket were those of Alma Tirtschke. We believed that all or most of them had been torn out or broken off near the nape when the blanket splayed back her glorious hair as the body was dumped near Gun Alley.

'Of course, Ross's defence would be caught off balance by novel evidence of this kind. But then it would deny our conviction that these were Alma's hairs. And it might counter with the proposition that the hairs fell from the head of one of the many other women known to have been willingly in Ross's little parlour nest while the blanket was there.

'If the defence could not produce a female witness with hair of identical colouring, it might try to confuse the jury by insisting that hairs which came from another part of a head could sometimes be darker than those found at the back. They might also assert the same doubts about the variable coarsenesses of human hair. We had to be absolutely positive. So Price and I resorted to strange tactics for responsible, allegedly respectable Crown scientists. We snooped on women in the city streets.

'Each lunch hour for several days we separately went down into the heart of Melbourne seeking women with crowning glories similar to Alma's lovely hair.

'I concentrated on Collins and Bourke Streets and the Centreway. Some days I did not strike one copperhead. At other times I would find two. It soon struck me that hair styles and fashions could easily enter this case. Alma had worn her hair in the schoolgirl's unpretentious, combed-down style. So hairs hanging down like hers would have been swept or torn out more easily than hairs from a head with the older, trussed-up style. But I wanted more than this. I wanted a point in pigmentation that would be unassailable.

'Price and I received some very bleak and haughty stares from red-haired women who turned suddenly in busy streets and found us peering closely at the napes of their necks. Some tried to call the police. It was embarrassing at times. But the embarrassment was worth while. Finally we had the shining answer. In the case of a copperhead there can be a slight, but scarcely noticeable, lightness in colour up near the bulb end of hairs at the nape.

'We had found that slight lightness of colour at the ends of Alma's hair – and of hairs on the blanket. In short, the hairs on the blanket had come from the nape of a female copperhead.

'The last conclusion we reached was that Alma's coarse hairs had the more positive and interesting pigment of a female of her age than of the similarly shaded hair of the ladies we had trailed. In other words, Alma's hair had real life in it.

'All these convictions, and the cardboard slides in our pockets, became the new-fangled evidence Mr Price and I were armed with when we attended the historic and dramatic trial of Colin Ross in the Criminal Court early in the autumn of 1922. We were well rehearsed to meet foreseeable challenges, ridicule and uproar that was to beat about us. For many hours behind the locked doors of our office Price practised giving evidence for the Crown with myself in the role of an astute and character-assassinating barrister.'

* * *

The fate of Colin Ross hinged on many things.

There were several submissions greatly in his favour. Among these was absence of any evidence at the earlier inquest that Alma had actually been seen in his saloon. Witnesses swore that Ross had told them he killed the girl. But then it was revealed that these witnesses were criminals who claimed to have heard Ross say this while he was awaiting trial at the old Melbourne Gaol in Russell Street. And the defence blasted them with imputations of giving false testimony in the hope of sharing a reward offered for incriminating evidence. A woman testified that Ross had confessed his guilt to her before he was arrested, but the defence came back with proof that she was an unreliable prostitute.

Into the spotlight next stepped the 'mystery woman' – striking, fair-haired Ivy Matthews. She swore that, as manageress of Ross's bar, she had been thoroughly conversant with his habits and routine, and that, on the day Alma died, she had seen the girl seated beyond the bead curtains of the private parlour. Ivy Matthews created a sensation in court as her testimony unfolded. But she refused to answer the many questions put by Ross's counsel as they challenged her lofty assertions that she was a woman of high repute.

Ross claimed, too, when the subject of human hairs was mentioned, that these must have fallen from the head of a Mrs Gladys Wain, who admitted she had been a frequent visitor to the saloon and had often combed her hair there.

Then Price and Taylor showed their hand.

Flatly they repudiated all suggestions that the hairs they now submitted could have come from the head of Mrs Wain. They took specimens of her hair. It was fine and golden. It bore no relationship whatever to those taken from the blanket and Alma's head.

Ross excitedly told the court he had been framed by the

police, and tension mounted when his barrister rose and begged to be disassociated from this unexpected outburst.

It seemed for a while that, although Ross's hopes had declined, the jury might have to decide whether the evidence of criminals, a prostitute, a 'mystery woman,' and the police reconstruction actually was sufficient to send a man to the gallows. Or, whatever they thought of all the evidence tendered, whether it would be overshadowed by the cold and measured opinions of the Government Analysts.

One thing is certain. The jury accepted the analysts' findings. The hairs on the blanket were those of Alma Tirtschke, who had been in Ross's saloon, and her body – despite his hot denials – had been in contact with a blanket removed from that saloon.

Ross was guilty and sentenced to be hanged at the old Melbourne Gaol opposite Victoria Police Headquarters.

While the jury was reading its verdict, the principal lay witness, Ivy Matthews, was given strong police protection night and day. But soon she vanished. Even Piggott, who knew her well, saw her only once. Before she disappeared she made a statement explaining why she had taken the role of a 'mystery woman' at the trial. This statement is interesting now because in Melbourne between 1959 and 1964 the Colin Ross case suddenly had strange echoes that went unheard by the general public.

This was Ivy Matthews' last message, given in 1922:

'During the hearing of the murder trial, Mr Maxwell, counsel for the defence, repeatedly referred to me as this "mystery woman" because he had failed to get from me many details of my past life. My silence in the witness-box has, no doubt, been the subject of a good deal of comment.

'Mr Maxwell had previously appeared for Ross in the arcade robbery case last November. On that occasion he held me up to the jury as a very reputable woman, and complimented me on the way I gave my evidence. But when I was not on his side he saw fit to discredit me in the eyes of the public.

'And now that I have given my evidence I want to reveal the real facts of my life, to let people know who "this mysterious Matthews woman" is.

'I was born at Burnie, Tasmania, on September 2, twenty-two years ago. My father died when I was three. I was nine years old when I was sent over to the mainland to help an aunt with housework until I was fifteen years old. It is an occupation I detested then and have detested since.

'My marriage – at eighteen – was none of my seeking.

'At that time I had it in mind to become a nurse.

'I had no real affection for my husband at the time. We lived together for just two weeks. I found that I had made a mistake. I had not the slightest fault to find with him. He was the personification of kindness, but I realised that we were badly matched.

'In December, 1920, I took a position at the arcade wine café, then conducted by a Mr and Mrs Lowe. I worked at the lolly shop in the morning and at the café in the afternoon. Colin Ross took over the business in April, 1921, and I continued to hold the two positions, getting thirty shillings a week from each.

'During Colin Ross's tenancy of the wine café I came into contact with all kinds of men including thieves and fences. These men gave me their confidences and I have never broken them. I used to have a very narrow outlook on life. I have never been what you call religious, though I was once a Christian Endeavourer.

'My experience in the wine bar has been a great education. I am a close student of human nature and I have learned to read a person at a moment's glance. I think that I am a better, not a worse, woman for that experience.'

Nearly forty years passed. Then, not long before he died, Mr Piggott again took up the case from where 'The Cat' had left the court. I told him I had talked with men who knew the late Mr T. C. Brennan, who had assisted Mr Maxwell in the defence of Ross, and others who often had discussed the case with Melbourne's brilliant barrister, Mr Jack Cullity, who had refused point-blank to appear for Ivy Matthews at the trial.

I explained that one barrister had said: 'Brennan told me, just before he died, that Ivy Matthews lied. He died believing implicity in the innocence of Ross and condemned completely the evidence of all lay witnesses.'

'Nevertheless,' said Piggott, 'there are several other factors not generally known which convinced us that the murderer was Colin Ross. I'll mention them now because, after all, it was the findings of Price and Taylor that put the rope around Ross's neck.

'First, we were certain Ross returned to his saloon late on the night of the murder because Italians living nearby saw lights on in his bar. Ross had gone home earlier that night to establish an alibi. On a tram he created a diversion by refusing to pay his fare. But Ross never knew the conductor had told us that, after he put Ross off, he saw Ross heading back towards the city – not towards Footscray. That is why Harold Saker travelled alternative routes so often.

'Second, after the inquest we found a billiards table brush in the scrub on a flat off the Footscray Road, near the Dynon Road bridge. This spot was not far from points where, earlier, the pieces of cloth positively identified as torn remnants of Alma's tunic had been found. On this brush we found a piece of the same material about five-eighths of an inch square. The reason this was not submitted as evidence at the trial is that it was found after the inquest. But I said to Ivy Matthews at the time: "Do you know if Ross owned a brush like this?" She told me Ross had such a brush and used it when grooming his pony at his house.

'We didn't doubt that for the brush had been struck many times with a curry-comb, a practice common among all mounted men. I didn't doubt, either, that this brush had been used to clean up the cul-de-sac when Alma's body was dumped there, because there were brush marks and other signs that the killer had tried to force the body down the drain, but had been disturbed.

'Ivy had said to me: "I don't think you need that evidence, Mr Piggott. I've got something that's almost an admission by Colin Ross." It was a letter said to be from Ross to his mother. Soon after I read it I met Mrs Ross in the Exhibition Gardens. She pleaded with me as a mother not to convict her son on his – or what she accepted as being his – own handwriting. I put it to the Crown prosecutor, and it was agreed that this letter should not be mentioned.

'Ross was hanged without the presentation of other evidence we could have given. When the case was over the witnesses went their own ways – "Staring Eyes," Ivy Matthews, Madame Gurkha and the rest. I have always believed Ivy was a good woman. I had no reason to think otherwise, although several persons claimed that she lied. But even if she did, I still believe the guilt of Colin Ross was indisputable. I did hear from Ivy once, but that was long, long ago. And I don't know what has happened to her since.'

Nor did I and others until one day in April, 1959, when we read a newspaper account of many persons fined heavily for evading income tax. It captured the attention of Detective-Sergeant Jack Ford, of the Homicide Squad, who later was to be the last policeman to see the 'mystery woman' alive.

This column proved that Ivy Matthews *did* become a nurse! There it was, in cold print, hiding a story that would be passed by millions:

'Irene Cholet. Nurse – failed to declare £16,000 between 1948 and 1956. Tax evaded, £3,681. Additional tax penalty, £1,840.'

The dossiers from police records left no doubt. The nurse was Ivy Matthews, one-time manageress of Ross's sleazy wine saloon, dogged defender of her name in court and print when Maxwell had bunched her in the 'quintet of reputables and disreputables,' the 'mystery woman' police had to guard, and one of 'the desperate people' who, Ross shouted to the judge, had 'sworn his life away.'

But this was the Ivy Matthews Ross never knew:

She was an abortionist. Her dossier number – 531/33 – records charges of abortion, receiving, unlawful possession and insulting words since 1933. Always she appeared in court under assumed names – Irene Cholet, Irene F. Sholet, Nurse Mack, Florence Mackie, Irene Mackie, Irene Smith and Patricia Cholet – that never revealed her true identity.

Her ageing generation and the younger students of criminal and legal history who shared their interest in the case believed her to be dead. Late in 1963, however, Jack Ford led a raid on a house at Kew, a superior suburb of Melbourne. They surprised a woman allegedly in the act of conducting grave illegal operations and charged her to appear before the Criminal Court. The hearing was delayed several times as the woman suffered repeated heart attacks. Finally it was listed for a Wednesday in September, 1964. Four days before this date the woman suffered another heart attack. She died the morning she was to have appeared in that court, prepared to admit her guilt in the name of Irene Cholet and go to gaol so that the case would be dealt with swiftly and her name, life and times as Ivy Matthews might never be revealed.

It is a story that could still arch more than an eyebrow here and there. One thinks how brilliant counsel again might flay the reputation of the Crown's chief lay witness if the hands of the clock could be turned back to that hot morning in court in 1922, when the damning words of Ivy Matthews and other witnesses were drowned for a time by one of the most violent and eerie thunderstorms that ever blasted Melbourne.

By her death Ivy Matthews wiped her own slate clean.

But whatever the judgment and opinion of today about the disputes in the Gun Alley Murder Case, the fact remains that Taylor's own case-book has solidly withstood the test of time.

2 Dull Gleam of Truth

LIKE the late Heath Robinson, Taylor always experimented with boyish enthusiasm to contrive gadgets from wire, string, pieces of tubing and wooden wheels. And he claimed, with an impish chuckle, that 'Anyhow, they worked!' Although he knew the melting-points of metals almost to a split degree, without his backyard escapism it could remain doubtful whether the great Walwa mysteries of the twenties and thirties ever would have been satisfactorily solved.

Only three persons could have denied the ensemble of chilling and accusing facts, and all are dead. They were dead twenty-six years ago, when an irritated coroner realised that frustration compelled him to leave an open verdict only because no one was alive to charge, or to sign, or even to contest the extraordinary evidence available to his court.

However, apart from a lack of vocal ghosts, there are no missing links now in this long and strange chain of events as gripping as any in the pages of Ellery Queen. This is the brand of real-life drama any crime reporter would like to cover or later reconstruct. It began about the time two dogs died because they had a taste for Australian bush stew and billy tea, and ended only when one echoing shot rang out on a hill that presides over the town of Albury, in New South Wales.

If the central figure in this story did not slay two women and try to poison his forest workmate before he was driven to suicide, then, as some of the original files in my possession prove, he left behind the greatest mass of damning circumstantial evidence known in Australasian police history.

Many view this case as one of Taylor's greatest contributions to scientific investigation because it was the complicated and scattered jigsaw puzzle which he and police had assembled laboriously and relentlessly which fired, by remote control almost, the one shot which ended a series of astounding mysteries in the lonely Australian bush.

Yet even after a tangle of doubts, lies, rumours and facts had been unravelled and evaluated, one experienced investigator apparently still doubted whether the sum of evidence was strong enough to have warranted a conviction for wilful murder. If he had substantial reasons for this difference of opinion, they are not known to the writer, or recorded. And certainly they never were evident to the other equally skilled investigators in agreement on the case.

This investigator was not implying that he questioned the guilt of the man they had in mind. According to his colleagues at the time, he merely questioned whether all the factual, scientific and circumstantial evidence would have led to the gallows. More intriguing are the incidents and inquiries that led to this debate.

There is no other comprehensive record of this outstanding case, not even among police files. The details which I present, through personal connections with the case and with many of its cast, are the only substantiated facts that have been recorded.

Even today there are fewer than a thousand folk among the beautiful and fertile valleys at Corryong, a peaceful agricultural and dairying township, in the far north-east of Victoria, which looks over the border of New South Wales to the snow-capped peaks of Australia's highest mountain, Kosciusko.

In the doldrum years after the First World War two men were employed as odd-jobbers on a dairy farm on the outskirts of this town. One, who said his name was White, was many years younger than the other. The older man did not trust White. Their task of repairing fences and digging postholes was not very rewarding, and White hinted more than once that all their work could be done by one man if the boss were prepared to pay a little more.

One night at their rough bush camp White brewed the billy tea and cooked the stew for both. But the older man morosely slouched off to his humpy bed after having taken only one mouthful from each tin dish. He had spat out both, grumbling that they were 'no good and bitter.' He left his dishes on the ground, close to the curled-up dogs nearby.

One of the dogs was fond of tea, and the other had a taste for stew. By morning both were dead. That was just as well for the older man. He was alive to the fact when he trekked into town and told the police. Ordinarily the deaths of two dogs would not have agitated them in that frontier-like region. But an urgent call for special attention was sent to the city because White had suddenly vanished from the mountains, and because it appeared that big doses of poison had been used by him.

'The Cat' was among the city experts who went to examine the dead dogs. His assignment was to determine whether poison had been used, and if so what kind. He found a few small crystals on the lip of a dish at the crude deserted camp. After studying them for a few moments he dipped a finger in the liquid remaining, and touched his tongue.

'Strychnine,' Taylor announced. 'But strychnine with this difference – it is coarse-grained. It is quite uncommon in Australia, and may easily have been brought into the country by someone who has been abroad. If and when a tin of it is found, we shall probably also find that it was packed in Madras. Whoever used it knew its potency and meant business.'

One of Australia's veteran homicide investigators was with Taylor that day.

'Taylor was dead right once more,' he recalls. 'We did find a tin, and it was labelled in Madras. We found White, too. We charged him, but he beat the rap. With little corroborative evidence the case was one that just would not stick in court.'

So White was freed. Officially he was a guiltless man. But his destiny was dark.

District old-timers such as Mr A. B. Post recall that the case caused a ripple of local interest for a time. But soon it was generally forgotten. The old bush labourer congratulated himself for not having eaten that 'terrible tucker,' and bought a beer all round.

Raymond Cyril White left the Corryong valleys and returned to Walwa, about twenty-five miles away. This peaceful district is a rugged fragment of the 1,600-square-mile Towong Shire. It is a mountainous dairying and timber region with fertile valleys and majestic plateaux watered well by permanent streams. White talked himself into farmhand work at 'The Pines', a 300-acre property five miles from Walwa township. It was owned by Elizabeth Brennan and her younger sister, Ellen Johanna, who preferred the name Johanna. The two had about sixty-four head of cattle and supplemented a comfortable living by breeding pigs and turkeys.

Johanna was then in her mid-thirties. White was younger, thirty-one, and the dominant characteristics of his everyday features were his small eyes, set wide apart, and a slack and uncertain mouth with a slight drag to the right. Elizabeth was forty-two and plain. She was short but weighed over twelve stone. She had bags under her eyes and folds under her chin, and the almost-disbelieving expression of a camel, besides suffering from ear trouble and catarrh. But Elizabeth did the talking. She was undisputed boss.

Apparently White was a man who appreciated a situation quickly, and could recover composure smartly after a rebuff. After working a few weeks at the farm he swore to Johanna that he loved her. But Johanna had never ignored the open suspicions and resentment voiced by her ageing parents, and she rejected him.

Unabashed, White re-applied the same principles of persistence and colossal nerve. They led him to the altar with plump, bespectacled Elizabeth.

Johanna hitched her skirts and huffed off to Queensland, several hundred miles to the tropical north. But she soon returned and resumed farm life as though there had been no rift or temporary parting of the ways. One day she made a will. She left her half-share of the farm to Elizabeth.

Months passed. Anzac Day came round – April 25, 1928. Throughout the Australian Commonwealth it was a public, almost sacred holiday. Why not also down on the farm? The three agreed. And so White and Johanna went to shoot fat ducks seen winging to a creek near the boundary of the farm.

Elizabeth saw her sister and husband set off together, little realising that she would never see her sister alive again.

Next day, at an inquest held locally by Mr H. P. McKenzie McHarg, she said:

'When he left the farmhouse my husband was carrying a bundle of rabbit traps, and my sister was carrying a single-barrelled gun. I last saw them passing the dairy. After they had been gone a few minutes, my husband ran into the house and said: "Come quick! Johanna was running along the bank with a gun when she slipped over and the gun went off and hit her."

'I immediately hurried with my husband to a washout in a gully about 250 yards from the house, where I saw the deceased lying. She had a wound behind the left ear and the gun was lying alongside of her. She appeared to be quite dead. I noticed a portion of the bank broken away as if something had fallen down it.

'I stayed with the body while my husband ran to Murray's for assistance. He returned some few minutes afterwards with Mr Wetmore, and they carried the body into the house.

'When I last saw the deceased she was in good spirits. There was no ill-feeling between either myself or my husband and my sister.'

Raymond White told the coroner that when he and Johanna were about 250 yards from the house, he saw two ducks fly past and alight farther up the gully.

'The deceased immediately loaded the gun and hurried up the gully in the direction of the ducks,' he said. 'I heard a faint click as she left me, which I think was her cocking the gun. She ran about a chain up the gully to the edge of a washout. I saw her go to the edge of the washout, and then I saw her fall and disappear into the washout.

'Almost immediately a shot rang out. I ran to the washout, which was about five feet deep, and I saw the deceased lying in the bottom with a large wound behind her left ear.'

Evidence was given by a constable. His statement is interesting and important because, years later, CIB headquarters was to demand a much more detailed report of the events and conclusions reached in that remote hamlet that day in 1928.

In his testimony to the coroner, the constable said he noticed that the bank of the washout was broken away as though someone had fallen down it. 'I saw blood at the bottom,' he said. 'In my opinion, the deceased in her excitement ran close to the edge of the washout, and the bank gave way and she fell over, the gun being discharged by the fall.'

The bush inquest concluded with this solemn declaration by the coroner: 'I say that Ellen Johanna Brennan died at Walwa on the 25th day of April, 1928, from the result of a gunshot wound accidentally inflicted, no blame being attached to any person.'

Johanna was buried that same evening and her small world soon forgot her.

Points to note at this stage are: Medical evidence from a qualified practitioner had not been given. White and his neighbour had improperly removed the body before any official had a chance to view the gun, the body, the positions of both persons at the scene.

But if these or other pertinent points were given serious thought by any in the district at that time – and I doubt it – no hint was included in official files. They lay dormant for almost eleven years, until they erupted with a burst that shook the hills.

Meanwhile, those hills slept on. White and his wife settled again to a life of work on the farm and an unexciting course of social outings with their friends.

Johanna had been dead just short of two years when the Whites' homestead burned down. It was rebuilt with the £1,400 claimed from the insurance company. But it was hardly surprising that some tongues in the district began to wag. Here and there sly references were made to 'that accidental shooting,' and we are told that cynical opinions circulated about 'that sudden fire that destroyed the whole of the building and every stick of furniture.'

Hawk-eyed country women are said to have noted with malevolent satisfaction that, although the fire had destroyed all the Whites' clothing, both were seen later wearing some of it in town. We are told that the local policeman became uneasy, too, and that he stayed that way for years. He had not seen Johanna's body in the washout because at the time he was out of town, but had told the coroner he believed her death was the result of an accidental fall.

If local rumours reached the hearing of the Whites there is no evidence that it vexed them. Certainly they did not affect their personal relationships, or those with their neighbours, because at the end of 1938 Elizabeth made another will. At this time she was the sole owner of a property worth at least £5,000, a small fortune for those times. She also had a substantial bank account, and her life had been insured for £1,000. She also owned a Plymouth car which was insured for £75.

By her original will, made about 1926, Raymond White was to have enjoyed only a life interest in her assets. But then Johanna was still alive. However, in December, 1938, Elizabeth made White joint-owner of her property and joint-drawer on her bank account.

White had come a long way since the stew-and-strychnine diet days of the 1920's. He was basking in the warmth and comfort of security. He was floating on a tranquil sea of submerged secrets that soon would be lashed by the force of a storm.

* * *

A few weeks later – it was about 9.40 p.m. on February 19, 1939 – White and Elizabeth were driving home along the lonely Shelley Road after having visited friends at the Jingellic butter factory.

White was driving.

The car reached a culvert in the road. A few minutes later it was burning furiously and plump Elizabeth was being reduced almost to ashes.

Raymond Cyril White was now sole owner of 'The Pines,' and he may have lived and died a man of substance and of widely accepted respectability had he reckoned more shrewdly with the forces that could be arraigned against him and his devilish plan.

Sadly that night, as he slumped by the overturned and furiously burning car, he jerked out his hazy recollections of the sudden crash that had changed his life.

'I saw a sheep standing on the right-hand side of the road,' White told the local constable. 'I was travelling at a speed of approximately twenty-five miles per hour at the time. Thinking that the sheep intended to run across the road, I steered the car to the left. When I tried to right the car back to the road, it did not answer the wheel. It travelled straight ahead and off the road. I felt a bump. I don't remember anything else till I saw the car on fire. I went to the car at once. It was upside-down, with the wheels in the air. I wrenched at the door and opened it. I saw my wife under the car. I got hold of her arm and tried to pull her out. I could not do so. The body under the car was the body of my wife.'

Albert O'Meally Hunt, a farmer who lived near the scene of the accident, had been the first to reach White that night. He said in his original signed statement:

'I remember the 19th of February, 1939. It was a Sunday. I was in bed asleep on the verandah. I heard a crash. I woke up and lay in bed, a few seconds later I heard somebody calling for help. I hopped out of bed, put on my trousers and boots and ran down to the road.

'I could see a faint light near the road. I ran down to where the light was, and I looked into a hole at the side of the road near the culvert, and I could see a motor-car in the hole, and it was on fire. As I got on the bank on the road I saw Mr White. He was dressed in a dustcoat and had a hat on. He said, "Come quick." We both jumped down the gutter and we went to the side of the car nearest the fence and I could see an arm sticking out.

'He picked up the arm. I caught hold of the arm. We pulled and I could see there was no hope of getting her out that way. I could see her shoulder. I could not see her face or her body.

'The door on the driving side was open about ten to eight inches. I did not pull the door. I then started to the cow yard for an axe. I then realised there was none there, after I had gone a chain. My brother Paddy arrived and he and White jumped down.

'The other doors were closed, all except the driving door. They both pulled the arm and I jumped down and White fell near the fire. I did not see him fall, but my brother called and with my brother we lifted White up on to the bank. I began to get frightened of an explosion of petrol. The fire was then burning fiercely.

'We then took White to our home. We got to the house at about 10.15 p.m. I estimate the time from what my brother told me. I went to bed at 9.30. So did my brother. He took the clock, and I only know it was 10.15 when we got home with White. From what my brother has since told me, we only have one clock and that clock would be in my brother's bedroom. It was in a room apart from the house. There would be no other clock in the house.

'I later went over to Mr Clyde's and on the way I met Vernon Brindley in a car and asked him to take White to hospital. He took him to hospital and he came back with Sister Robinson and Constable Orr. Sister is an ex-bush nurse.

'When I went down to the fire first, White said: "Come quick," or something to that effect. My brother asked White what happened and White said: "The steering went crook" or went bung or failed, or something to that effect. White never made any effort to cut any upholstery or anything else while I was there.

'After we pulled the arm, he rushed down and pulled or dragged at something, but after that I thought I saw some red on his arm which I took for blood. That was the only blood I saw.

'I saw a rug and a grey sports coat near the fence on the bank near where the car was burning, and a torch was with them. They were just lying on the bank. I went past the scene about 7.30 a.m. on the 20th (the morning after the accident) and the rug and sports coat were still lying on the bank of the gutter. I never touched anything.

'I saw the rug lying over where the corpse was about 9 a.m. I heard somebody say it was not a very good sight for people to look at and it was after that that the rug was thrown over the corpse. I have never conversed with White about it since that night. He has been staying at our place for two or three days since he came out of hospital. I have never heard any quarrels between White and his wife, but I would say she was boss.'

Those were typical of several statements made to Mounted

Constable Allan Vernon Orr, of Walwa. The State-wide Victorian Criminal Investigation Branch, then in process of reorganisation and redistribution by the new police chief, Alex Duncan, and the new CIB chief Detective-Superintendent Robert Dower, was then centred mainly in and around the Melbourne metropolitan area. Country branches were about to be founded, but none had been established in the far north-west when this case began. Orr, therefore, was man-on-the-spot during the few days when the first faint but persistent doubts were raised.

His stabs of uneasiness, which helped to accelerate the probe at higher level, seem to be reflected in some passages of his report:

'About 10.20 p.m. on Sunday, February 19, 1939, I was at the police-station, Walwa, when a Mr Clyde informed me that Mr White's car had capsized on the Shelley Road, opposite Hunt's place. He had taken White to the bush nursing hospital at Walwa and thought Mrs White was in the car that was burning. I accompanied him to the scene of the accident. I saw Mr White's car turned upside-down in a washaway on the left-hand side of the road near a culvert. The washaway is about ten feet deep at the deepest end.

'The car was in the washaway between the culvert and the fence. It was burning fiercely from the dashboard back towards the rear of the car. The door on the driver's side of the car was partly open. This was on the right side of the car. The other side front door was closed. The two rear doors were closed.

'I saw a body under the burning car, lying on its back, face upwards, with the head near the driving side door that was partly open. The chest was under the steering column. The other side of the body seemed to be under the frame of the front seat, which was burnt and lying on the body. The floor-boards were burnt when I got there. This made it possible to see the position of the body.

'Albert Hunt, Patrick Hunt, Vernon Brindley and Sister Robinson were there at the time. With the Hunt brothers, I secured some water and put the fire out as well as we could. The body was then practically ashes and unrecognisable.

'I examined the road for wheel or tyre tracks, and about

fifteen yards back from the culvert, on the opposite side of the road to the car, I saw the tracks of a car bearing to the left straight across the road in a diagonal direction – straight to where the car had gone over the table drain and continued up the bank between the fence and the washaway, where the marks stopped.

'This appeared to be the spot where the car had tipped sideways into the washaway, coming to rest at the bottom of the washaway on its hood with the wheels up.

'There was no indication of any skid marks or of the brakes having been applied. The marks appeared to be consistent with the wheels at the rear having tracked the front wheels. The marks on the roadway went in a straight line to where it had overturned.

'There were no wobble marks. I examined the steering of the car and it appeared to be in good order and workable. There did not appear to be in any defect. I saw that the gears were seized. The grey sports coat produced I found on the bank near the fence between the washaway and the fences. The right side of this coat was bloodstained. I found a torch in the coat pocket and I found another large torch on the bank near the coat. A felt hat was found and placed in the car in which I was travelling.

'I did not see any sheep or sheep tracks about.

'The fire when I first saw it was burning fiercely from the dashboard back towards the rear of the car. I left the scene about 1 a.m. I left everything in the same condition as when I found it. I returned the next morning and again inspected the wheel tracks on the road which went across a table drain to where the car had tipped over into the washaway.

'I could not see any sign of any skid marks or brake marks along the tracks made by this car.

'With assistance, the car was lifted on to its side, and from under where the car had been I saw the remains of a body. With assistance it was placed in a coffin and taken to Walwa, where it was examined by Dr Greenham, of Corryong.

'I took possession of a handbag, catch, a chain, a small knife, a wristlet watch, some silver and copper coins, all of which had been burnt in the fire.

'I interviewed White at the bush nursing hospital. I said to him: "How did the accident occur?" He said: "I was driving along the Shelley Road when I saw a sheep on the road. I thought it was going to run in front of me. I steered the car to the left. The sheep stopped where it was, and when I tried to steer the car to the right the steering jammed and the car careered off the road. The next thing I knew I felt a big bump."

'I said: "What did you do then?" He said: "I rushed round to the side door, wrenched it open, and tried to pull my wife out. But I could not move her so I also called for help."

'I said: "Is it possible that you went to sleep?" He said: "Oh, no. I was talking to my wife all the time."

'I examined the clothing that had been removed from him when he was admitted to hospital. It had been washed. There were no signs of any cuts or tears in the clothing.

'Dr Greenham examined White. I took a written statement from White which he signed. He did not appear to be unduly upset. I asked him if he had the car insured and he said: "Yes, only for a small amount." I said: "How much?" He said: "I think it was £70."

'I know the Shelley Road well.

'Between Walwa and the residence of White, the washaway in which the car capsized is the only one on that road in which a car could be completely overturned.'

Whether the body should have been removed that dark night of the accident or left until the light of day is a matter of opinion. An angry and admonishing coroner was one of those who later were to take the view that it should have been removed and examined immediately in case, by then, the heat had not reduced it to the charred remains that left few clues.

This, however, could be wisdom well after the event. It does not appear to allow for the limited resources in that remote part of the bush. And certainly there would have been no reason or room for criticism or complaint but for the amazing revelations that lay ahead.

At police headquarters, nearly three hundred miles away, it was soon apparent that although many of the circumstances reported could be consistent with a fatal accident, there were contradictions and a haziness which warranted a balanced investigating team being sent to Walwa to dig for unpleasant facts. It was true that the surgeons at Walwa had found no evidence that Mrs Elizabeth White had died from anything but accidental burns. There were several other features reasonably in line with the accident White had described. But there seemed to be intriguing inconsistencies as well.

A mounted trooper, bred to Australian bush life, had found no sheep tracks or any other sign of sheep on or near the Shelley Road. There were no skid marks, as might have been expected on that road. Several experienced bushmen had testified to that. The car had overturned at the only point on a very long and lonely road where that was possible. And so on.

And there were the hunches good detectives get when there could be other facts to be unearthed – perhaps literally. Who was White? What did the Police Department know about him?

The routine check produced the constable who had given evidence at Johanna's inquest eleven years earlier. This time he said:

'I had wanted to have the inquest adjourned, but the deputy-coroner was quite satisfied about it and decided to go on with the inquest and finished it off before the burial.'

Indeed! Was that a fact? Headquarters police sat bolt upright.

The constable continued: 'Some time after that rumours began to fly about regarding the shooting, but nothing tangible could be gathered. Some few years after this a fire occurred in White's dwelling house on their farm, and the building and furniture were totally destroyed. I reported on the matter, giving some grounds for suspicion, but I cannot recollect now exactly what it was, and the report was returned to me for further report as to the result of the insurance adjuster's inquiry. The adjuster was satisfied and ridiculed me for my suggestion that the fire was suspicious, and I reported to the effect that the adjuster was satisfied, and there the matter lay.

'Rumours were current after the fire that this was not a genuine accidental fire, and some of their clothing that was supposed to have been burnt in the fire was seen some months afterwards being worn by White and his wife. It was apparent that the wife and husband were parties to this fire.

'From my inquiries I felt that, if the fire was wilfully set that day, it was done by Mrs White because the husband was supposed to be with another man working down on the bank of the creek a considerable distance from the house when the fire began, while the wife, she drove a horse and jinker to a neighbour's place – called Hunt – and had just reached there when the fire was first noticed. Her demeanour and actions at the time were suspicious.

'White bought a Plymouth tourer while I was at Walwa. I did not know anything about the insurance on the car. I did not know of the Whites quarrelling or having any domestic differences.'

But, as the constable said, there the matter lay, until eleven years later when the headquarters squad was speeding up to the cool mountains of the border. Among them were Detective-Inspector Harry (the Wolf) Carey, Detective-Sergeant Fred Sickerdick (later chief of the Railways Investigation Branch), Detective Fred Delminico, the Government pathologist Dr Crawford Mollison, and the Government Analyst Mr Charles Anthony Taylor.

Another long statement from White was recorded by Delminico in longhand in a blue threepenny notebook. Sometimes that statement seemed to strike a note of truth. Sometimes it was disarming and convincing. And yet, in many ways, it appeared to be a strange and rambling statement, possibly because Delminico was determined to sift it over and over again.

Here, published for the first time, is the full text of the statement taken directly from that simple notebook, a statement that set the police thinking hard:

'I have been living at Walwa for about sixteen years,' White told Delminico. 'I came to Walwa from Narrandera (in New South Wales). I am a native of South Africa. I have been in Australia nineteen or twenty years. I came out on . . . I can't think of the name of the boat.

'I have no relatives in Australia. I landed at Port Melbourne. I am a returned soldier. I was with the Cape Rifles, No. 1642, of South Africa. I enlisted at Durban. I was discharged in

Africa. I was on service in Africa. My battalion was the 17th Foot Battalion. I have not got a discharge or medals. I am not associated with any soldiers' association. I was born at Glencoe, South Africa. I was twenty-six when I came to Australia. I was a labourer by occupation.

'I was on service in German East Africa for about three years. The commander was General Vanderwenter. I first worked at Melbourne. I bought a spring cart, and with another man I set off to trap rabbits and went to Narrandera. I worked at Barrowye station for about four years. Mr John Houston was the manager. From there I came to Walwa. I met my late wife at a sports meeting at Walwa. I was married to her on November 11, 1925, at St. Patrick's Cathedral, Albury.

'I then worked for various people for the first six months. The farm was leased. After the lease expired we went and worked and lived on the farm. The farm comprises about three hundred acres and is worth about £10 an acre. It was about six or seven months from the date of my arrival in Australia until I went to work on Houston's station.

'I came straight to Australia from Africa. When we went to the farm we took up dairying. There was a sister of my wife's there also. She met with an accident and died about ten years ago. It was an accident with a shotgun. She fell down a bank and the gun went off. It was a single-barrel gun. I think it was burnt in the fire when the house was burnt down. The wife and I carried on the farm. The farm belonged to the two sisters. When my wife's sister died my wife became the owner of the property. The sister left her share of the property to my wife by will.

'The wife and I carried on the dairying and we done most of the work. We have machinery and have milked up to sixty-four cows. We employed labour from time to time. The cream was sent to the Jingellic factory.

'My wife was aged fifty-six years. My age is forty-five years. The wife and I got on well. In fourteen years we never separated for a week. We worked together. We never quarrelled and we had no domestic differences. The property, prior to my wife's death, was held by my wife and I as joint tenants. The title was transferred in the joint names of my wife and I about

October, 1938. The business was arranged through Mr Harman, Bank of New South Wales, Walwa, and Mr Anderson, solicitor.

'This was brought about through me putting labour and money into the place. I had over £200 when I married and I had put in all the labour after marriage, and the wife went to Mr Harman and asked to arrange the transfer of title into our joint names. He got in touch with Mr Anderson, who drew up the title. I did not suggest anything to the wife to get the transfer. She suggested that it be done. I considered it a waste of money – I think it cost £30.

'My solicitor has the will my wife left. She left the property to me in the will. The will was made ten to twelve years ago, shortly after marriage. I also made one in favour of my wife at the time. Mr Teitchen, of Albury, drew up the will. There were other conditions in the will of my late wife. There was £100 for a church fund. I cannot remember other amounts.

'I am the sole executor of the will. On the 19th of February I was with my wife at a picnic at Jingellic with Mr and Mrs Corbett. We went there about 5 p.m. Miss Hollow, the book-keeper from the butter factory, and a Mr Joe Corbett were at the gathering. We remained until about 7.30 p.m. We then went to Mr Corbett's place and remained until 9.40 p.m. The man who is the book-keeper told us the time, and after saying goodnight to Mrs Corbett we left there at 9.45 p.m.

'The wife and I were alone in the car. I think Mrs Hollow and the book-keeper left about the same time. I drove straight home through Walwa and up the Shelley Road. There were a number of cars about Walwa. I was driving along, and when I got opposite Hunt brothers' property there was a sheep on the right-hand side of the road. I was travelling about thirty miles an hour.

'The car was a Chrysler Plymouth with folding seat, a touring model. I swerved to the left as the sheep had started to run across the road. I swerved away from the sheep to the left. When I tried to right the car it did not respond. The car did not straighten up. There was something wrong with the steering. The car continued straight on off the beaten track and hit the rough ground caused by the table drain.

'It bounced violently and plunged into the ditch. I left the car when I got the shock of the first bump. The shock of the bump hurled the door open. I was thrown out on the road near a post. I think I landed on my right side. I scrambled into the ditch when I saw the car upside-down in the ditch.

'I rushed to the front of the car from the back to see if my wife had been thrown out. I wrenched the door on the driving side off. I could see my wife under the wreck. I tried to get her out. She appeared to be jammed. I pulled some things like clothing – such as a tablecloth and towel – out and I could not see her limbs to catch hold of until I did this. I then saw her arm and reached in and freed it. I think it was her right arm. She appeared to be dead. I called to her several times, "Lizzie . . . Lizzie," but I got no answer.

'I did not hear her groan as the car left the road. She said: "What is wrong?" or "Where are we going?" She did not scream or, as far as I know, she did not catch hold of the steering wheel. After I caught hold of her arm and tried to pull her out; it was a folding seat and it was held by a strap. I then tried to undo the strap and could not. I caught the top of the car and kicked at it to try to undo or break the strap. I then got my knife and slashed the strap through and then tried to pull her from under the wreck.

'A fire had started in the engine under the bonnet. It had not reached back into the car and was not burning fiercely. The fire had got a good hold by the time I had tried to get my wife free from the wreck. The whole time I was trying to get my wife I was calling: "Help! . . . help!"

'Mr Albert and Pat Hunt then arrived and they tried with me to get the wife from under the car. By this time the fire was burning the body part of the car and was burning fiercely. We could not get her out, and then somebody said the petrol tank will go up. Then we backed to the rear of the car and I fell over and Mr Hunt dragged me out, and I looked back and saw flames around my wife in the fire. I tried to rush in to get my wife and the Hunt brothers held me from doing so. The knife I was using to cut the strap and part of the car – I probably threw it down somewhere.

'I was then taken to Hunts' home. They would not let me

go there any more. It was about 10.10 p.m. when I reached Hunts' home. It was that time by Hunts' clock. I was later taken to hospital. I know the time because the clock was right opposite me in the room at the Hunts' house.

'That night I was dressed in a dustcoat, a coat shirt, an ordinary singlet, a pair of trousers, socks and shoes. I had a sports coat in the car but it was not being worn by me. It was a grey colour. As far as I know, it was burnt.

'It was an ordinary knife (answering one of Delminico's sharp questions) with a sharpened blade.

'I was taken to hospital by Mr Vic Clyde and Vernon Brindley in a car. I had a cut in the left forearm, slight cut in the right leg near the ankle, large bruise under right breast, bruise on left shoulder, gravel rash on right hip, sore back and stomach pains, and slight scratches on the chest. I don't think they bled. None of the cuts needed stitching.

'I hope you won't get annoyed, but my solicitors advised me not to say how I got them.

'The marks on the chest were, I believe, caused when I got hold of the door and wrenched it off. It was holding by one hinge and I wrenched it violently, and when it came off the edge of it struck me in the chest and caused the scratches. The cut on the left arm was caused when I tried to cut the strap holding the seat. It did not cut through the first time. It was in an awkward position and the fire was getting hot. I got right down on my knees and seized the strap with the left hand and held it tight. I slashed vigorously with the knife in the right hand and the knife cut through the strap and ran along the arm and caused the cut.

'When I was kicking the strap, trying to break it, I had hold of the top portion of the car and kicked as hard as I could. On one occasion I missed the strap. My foot shot through and I think it ran along the buckle and scratched the leg above the ankle. The strap was the one holding the seat.

'The bruise and gravel rash on the right side I got, I believe, when I was thrown out. Dr Worch, of Albury, examined me on the 27-2-39 and he told me I had an internal injury and it would necessitate an operation. He said it was an injury from the accident and that, owing to bruising, he would not operate.

'My shirt and singlet were worn open by me that night. It was a very warm night. My wife was wearing a light coat frock, blue colour, with light colouring in it. I think she had light shoes, light blue hat to match the dress. She was a stout woman about twelve stone. She was about five foot six inches high. She had general good health. She had no chronic illness. She had been attended by Dr Jeffries, Tallangatta. I think it was a catarrh complaint, and she also visited a doctor in Corryong for catarrh and ear trouble.

'The chap I was with when I first went trapping was Thomas McPhee. The last I knew of him he was going to New Guinea.

'I was in Melbourne in 1924 and I was there again in 1928. The car is my property and insured for £70. It is a comprehensive policy. The agent for the Federation Company told me that, being a country man and not driving in the city, they would give me better conditions. I paid £5 a year to cover policy. I received concessions for being a country member not driving in the city – lowering of premium. My wife was not insured. My sister-in-law was not insured. My father's name was Mathew White. He died thirty-five years ago in South Africa. My mother died about thirty years ago – Mary White. I am the only child. I don't know my mother's maiden name.

'I started with Cape Light Horse and later went into the infantry. I attended the State School at Glencoe, South Africa.

'Sister Hills was a bush nurse at Walwa. Sister Fairweather was a nurse at Walwa. I am not sure which of them attended the sister-in-law who was shot.

'The car was in top gear when I was driving along the road. I never put it in second gear. I have an idea I put the foot on the brake when it started to leave the road. I did not put on the hand brake.

'The door I pulled off was the door on the driving side in front. The other three doors were closed. The door I pulled off I threw on the ground. The clothes I was wearing were at the hospital for some time. I destroyed them after I collected them from hospital. I burnt them. I also had all my wife's clothes burnt.

'I have an old Savage rifle and a .303 rifle and a breechloader single barrel – it is a single barrel. I bought it last year.

'The lights on the car on the night of the smash were in good order and were alight. The rug, billy tin and the enamel billy, sports coat and the singlet are my property. The coat and singlet I had with me the night of the tragedy.

'I burnt the trousers – blue ordinary trousers – a coat shirt, I burnt on Saturday last, the 25-2-39, and I also burnt some of the wife's clothes that were in the home. I would say that there was about six gallons of petrol in the car at the time of the smash.

'I had been in to Albury on 15-2-39 and filled up. The tank would hold eleven gallons of petrol. I drove the car home. I used the car next Sunday, the 19th. I drove straight to Jingellic and was returning when the smash occurred. That was the only travelling I did on that tank of petrol. I believe there would be six gallons left.

'In 1919 – I don't know the month – I embarked at Durban on a boat. I don't know the name. I got a passport. I got my photo taken at a shipping office, a place they had at the wharf. I got the photo and passport taken there.

'I was working for Voorst at Ladysmith, about fourteen miles out, for about twelve months at 22s. 6d. a week. Voorsts were farmers. I worked my passage out. I was a general deck hand. A man named Campbell was a mate on the boat.

'I got the passport at the employment bureau. I got the job from the mate, Campbell. I have not been in any country other than South Africa and Australia.

'The clothes I burned were those associated with the tragedy.'

That is a statement to be read carefully. Here and there it shows how an investigator, professionally suspicious and uneasy, suddenly reverts to points which, at first sound and glance, appear to have been answered. Even White's vagueness on some points could have been understandable due to possible shock and the lapse of time. Some of the detail is convincing enough, and there are not many gaps. But there are discrepancies – or are they only oversights? – and these alerted Delminico and the other detectives.

Detective-Superintendent Dower said at the time that he

found it difficult to accept that a man could not recall the name of a ship that had brought him to Australia seeking a great adventure.

'I cannot accept his account of his service in Africa, a theatre I know well,' he said. 'It has a hollow ring, more like the echo of another man's story.'

The men on the job agreed. They redoubled their efforts to check White's claims.

A garage mechanic told them that the brakes of White's car had been in excellent order because he had examined them not long before the accident. However, White had not been as positive about using the brakes as he had about the 'crook' steering, which apparently – but who could prove it? – had been in good working order.

At this stage the detectives were more interested in the clothes White had worn that night, in the few articles that had not burned, and in the minor injuries he claimed to have suffered while his wife was dying. These points, pressed home very hard, offered a more promising total:

Point 1. White had suffered several sharp cuts on his chest *beneath* his singlet. But that singlet, one of the items he had not burned, was *not* torn or cut.

Point 2. When White's statement was checked at the local surgery the doctor said those cuts were 'almost perfect examples' of self-inflicted wounds.

Point 3. The same doctor added that, when he had examined White after the accident, he had not found any traces of the gravel rash he would have expected to see on a man who claimed he must have been hurled from a moving car.

Sceptical and implacable, the police and the scientists turned off on another tack. They exhumed the body of Mrs Elizabeth White and examined it for three grisly hours. But even the quite outstanding Government pathologist of the day still found it impossible to certify what had caused death. Yet it happened to be during that disappointing examination of the charred remains that Charles Anthony Taylor was given the fleeting opportunity of seeing the first dull gleam of the dreadful truth.

A small and tarnished fragment, apparently heavy for its

size, fell from the remains and rattled across the timber floor. Taylor thought it was a stone at first, but saw it had a faint gleam. He picked it up and rubbed it on his sleeve.

Lead? No. Of all things, it was a small scrap of more expensive metal. Gold. It was only about half an inch long and an irregular quarter of an inch wide, and it was roughly the shape of a banana. Taylor was still cradling it thoughtfully in his palm when the pathologist and his assistants again failed to conclude whether Mrs White had died as a result of burns, accident injuries, or possibly knife wounds, bullets, strangulation or some other means.

This surely was one of the most provocative but stimulating periods of Taylor's life.

Men like to wonder, and that is the seed of our science. Emerson wrote this many years ago, probably having men of Taylor's calibre in mind.

Taylor was in fact still wondering when the pathologist and staff attendants left and he was alone with the tiny nugget. Why did it bring a glint to his grave eyes, and that characteristic lift to the corners of his mouth? Why did he stiffen, breathing hard, and stare out towards the purple crags, lost in profound thought?

'Because,' he revealed to me long after the event, 'I knew all the properties of gold from those times when I had fossicked for just tiny specks of it on those mullock heaps of Maryborough as a kid, and I had learned a lot about its changing qualities as a scientist since then.

'I knew that what had fallen at my feet from the corpse was not a morsel of alluvial gold. It could not have been a tiny nugget of raw gold. I knew that the whole of the Towong Shire we were in was noted for its fertility, its grazing pastures, its fat lambs and pigs, its rich milk and butter, and – in parts – deposits of tin.

'But gold? Natural gold? No, upon my soul! I could only have been holding processed gold – a small, almost shapeless mass that once had been a brooch or other ornament, and most likely a wedding-ring – that had melted in the blaze.

'I was certain there wasn't a chance that it could have been a nugget from the top layers of the earth when the woman's body had been taken from the wreckage or brought up from her grave. So, when I looked again at the near-shapelessness of that little mass, and found no sign of a wedding-ring among the woman's remains, I knew – though possibly it was a little early to be quite sure – that Elizabeth White was the victim of a clever, extraordinary and premeditated murder. Right at that moment I convinced myself that we could uncover one of the strangest, most careful and most diabolically cold-blooded murder plots in my experience.

'I was confident, then, that we would find an answer to all the riddles of the bush somewhere among the wreckage of that car. I was equally certain, too, that Mrs White had been deliberately killed – stabbed, perhaps, but more probably shot – *before* the car was engulfed in flames, and I was hoping that if we examined that "crash" scene again we might find evidence to prove it.'

Early next day the tireless Delminico and his team began to dig and sieve the dry, scorched earth and cold embers where the driving seat of the car had been. Several hours passed before these monotonous efforts were rewarded by tiny flashes of reflected light at the bottom of a sieve. They were silver flashes from two pieces of metal smaller than the gold.

They were spent lead bullets of .22 calibre.

However, there had not been any medical evidence of bullet marks among Mrs White's remains, one detective pointed out. There were not even scratches on her bones. So, assuming White was innocent, how did the bullets come to be there?

One of the local farmers had recollected that, before he had run to the burning car that night, he had heard something like cartridges being fired, and later had assumed they had exploded in the flames.

Almost everyone in the Australian bush carried cartridges of some kind in their car, especially cartridges for, say, a .22 rifle, the detectives also pointed out. Circumstantially, finding these spent bullets might not help White's case. But, all considered, it was unlikely that this evidence without medical backing would have much weight in court. It would be discounted when the doctors confirmed there had been no bullet scorings on the bones.

But 'The Cat' and others held different views. He reasoned this way: If, in fact, a fair number of cartridges had exploded, why was there only this trace of them? The soil had been thoroughly sieved and this was the only evidence it yielded. Was it conceivable that there were only two .22 cartridges in that car? Assuming that a box had exploded – or part of a box – was it acceptable that these two bullets were, by the very longest arm of coincidence, to be found inches down in the earth and absolutely in the spot where the woman's body had been? Wasn't it significant that no cartridge cases had been found – not even two? Didn't this presuppose that only two bullets had been expended at the scene, and that they were fired from a gun to bore down in that earth?

Taylor looked at the bullets closely before he announced his considered opinion.

'I say Mrs White was carefully and deliberately shot through the heart,' he said. 'That would explain why there are no foreign scorings on the bones. See this small brown stain on this little bullet? I'll stake my reputation that this is human blood.'

Later tests proved him right.

Taylor then played his trump card.

'The police had been tirelessly dragging little bits of information and possible evidence from the locals day after day,' he explained to me. 'They were outstandingly patient and tenacious. Why was his sports coat bloodstained? they had asked repeatedly. How did he manage to save the rug found on the embankment later? Where was the knife he said he used, but which apparently no one else saw during his alleged efforts to free his wife? What was that empty one-gallon petrol tin doing in the long grass not far from the overturned car? And so on.'

Taylor told me how he scrambled down into the culvert ditch and viewed the wreckage for several minutes.

'I know the evidence isn't tight enough to warrant a murder charge,' he told one group on the spot. 'But there's one sure way to tighten it. We should prove that whoever killed Mrs White had a sound knowledge of engineering principles. I would say the killer is one who had been an artificer in a ship's engine room, possibly in the merchant service, maybe in the Navy. Certainly during recent times.'

He outlined his reasons for this conclusion. It was a long way from the cool uplands of the border to the throbbing plates of a ship at sea. The hypothesis seemed incredible. But the detectives, throughout long years of liaison, knew Taylor's uncanny facility to bridge gaps between events and facts.

They went to work with renewed vigour.

Frederick William Delminico was convinced that White was worth another visit, and that any uneasiness on his part should be allayed while a fresh effort was made to uncover any secrets in his life.

This was the report Delminico, after days of hard work, submitted to headquarters of the Victorian CIB:

'With White we went to his home, where he pointed out some ashes where he had burnt the clothing he was wearing at the time of the tragedy. I took possession of some of the ashes and handed them to Mr Taylor, the Government Analyst.

'We made a search of White's house with White, but nothing of an incriminating nature was found. After further inquiries we returned to Melbourne.

'Inquiries there disclosed that Raymond Cyril White was married at Albury to the deceased, Elizabeth Ann White, *née* Brennan, on 11/11/1925. Copy of certificate of marriage produced.

'I later obtained the birth certificates of Elizabeth Ann White and Ellen Johanna Brennan.

'I inspected the titles at the Titles Office of Property Val. 5522 Folio 1104223 and ascertained that the title had been transferred from the name of Elizabeth Ann White and Raymond Cyril White, the transfer being registered on 9/12/38.'

Delminico began one of the greatest Australian searches and cross-checks ever made through records of Government bureaus. With commendable restraint he wrote:

'After information had been received, my inquiries disclosed that an Edgar Joseph Raymond Farrell was one of a family of ten, his father being Martin Farrell and his mother Mary Farrell – *née* White. On the death of that man's father, certain property was divided among the children, and inquiries have disclosed that £70 is held on behalf of Edgar Joseph Raymond Farrell by Public Trustees, Sydney.'

Delminico knew he had reached the brink of an astounding discovery when he continued: 'An Edgar Farrell had deserted the Royal Australian Navy on 9/10/1919. I then searched the *Police Gazette*. I ascertained that a warrant had been issued for the arrest of Edgar Farrell as a naval deserter in October, 1919 (naval record produced). The warrant was cancelled after three years. It was ascertained from this issue of the *Gazette* that Farrell was born at Corowa, New South Wales, and I produce the birth certificate of Edgar Joseph Raymond Farrell.'

So 'White' was Farrell!

The descriptions tallied. Five foot six and a half inches, dark hair, blue eyes, two scars on left knee. The date of birth was identical – 18/4/1894.

While being questioned earlier White had given his mother's correct maiden name, Mary White, and this was one of the points Delminico had not overlooked as he began his mammoth check of records and files.

It was also clear from records that White had never been to South Africa. His father or brother had died at Johannesburg during the South African War, and it seems that his references to that country and its people must have stemmed from remembered family conversations in happier days. Records did show, however, that under his true name, Farrell, he had joined the Royal Australian Navy on 26/2/1914. He was in London between October, 1915, and January, 1916, and deserted from Jervis Bay naval station, New South Wales, on 8/10/1919.

And to Taylor's delight his record proved that his naval rank was engine-room petty-officer!

For twenty years after he deserted he had kept the deception and mystery of his disappearance from his large family and even from Elizabeth, the wife they never met.

Detectives who traced his relatives found they thought him dead. One was his married sister, of Alma Road, St. Kilda, Melbourne. Until her brother vanished they had been on very friendly terms.

'All the family's efforts to trace Edgar Farrell have failed for years,' the detectives reported. 'During the time he was in the Navy he corresponded regularly with his sister. But soon after the Great War he left the Navy. His reason for doing so is unknown. He and Mrs Vial were always more closely associated than other members of the family. He wrote to her more regularly. They were always on the best of terms and she cannot give an explanation why he would disappear and not write.

'The Public Trustees, Sydney, were the executors of his father's will, and when it was being executed all efforts to trace Edgar Farrell proved useless. He was advertised for in newspapers throughout the world, but he could not be located and the executors hold about £100 on his behalf.

'They also hold the same amount on behalf of his brother, who is still reported missing at Lone Pine, Gallipoli, 1915.'

The net around Edgar Farrell, *alias* Raymond White, was being drawn very close.

When the police team reassembled in the Walwa district after their success in Melbourne, they prepared to search White's property and the culvert more closely. With grim satisfaction they dragged, from the bottom of one of the deep dams on White's farm, a .22 pistol weighted with a heavy piece of iron. Fingerprints had been destroyed while it was submerged, but even without ballistics tests the police knew it had been discharged in recent weeks. They knew, too, although White had refused to admit it when interrogated, that he had owned a weapon of this calibre.

Did White hear of this dramatic find? We never can be sure, although his reactions suggest he did. But one can be sure it was his fear of the hunt exposing his Jekyll-Hyde existence that prompted him suddenly to seek his own way out.

Police were on their way to arrest him when he vanished. Then the manhunt was really on.

This message was flashed from Victorian CIB headquarters to the Sydney Central CIB:

'Will you please have expresses and other trains met which leave Albury for Sydney today and tomorrow with view to tracing man named Raymond Cyril White believed identical with Edgar Farrell your gazette 1919 page 545 stop also check on all planes stop description 45 years five feet six or seven inches dark hair blue eyes sallow complexion receding chin clean-shaven wears dark or grey suits stop he had been farming at Walwa Victoria stop his wife had met her death in a motor-car burnt in suspicious circumstances stop if located please shadow him and keep him under surveillance and let me know end Dower Superintendent.'

But White was never seen in Sydney. He was not seen alive again. He had fled to Albury, the hustling town on the New South Wales–Victoria border. At the base of the returned soldiers' monument, on the hill that broods over the lovely town, he scribbled his last words and gazed out to the border ranges that had held his dreadful secrets for so long. Then he killed himself with a shotgun blast.

He fell as Detective-Sergeant Frederick Sickerdick was combing the town for him.

Carey and Delminico viewed his body at the Albury morgue, and if there had been a lingering doubt about his dual personality they erased it there.

'I examined the body,' Delminico reported, 'and I found the scars identical with those of the Navy Department's description of Edgar Farrell.'

That was almost the end of an extraordinarily dogged and tiring manhunt. It was the sequel to long chapters of duplicity, cunning and intrigue which may never have been revealed if small but vital errors had not been made and deadly trifles had not been dug from the neutral bush.

White was normally a cool thinker. In different circumstances he may have succeeded with his long-range plan. He could have inherited a small fortune and perhaps returned to his family later with a convincing story of travel and success abroad.

His plot remains as one of the most crafty and neatly executed in the records of Australian police. But his fatal error was to underestimate the resources and intelligence of the police and their scientist allies. Although suspicion snowballed against him after a halting start, he may have thwarted or deceived his enemies if he had carried away a one-gallon petrol tin found not far from the overturned car; removed his wife's wedding-ring as carefully as, it is supposed, he picked up the two cartridge cases ejected from his pistol when his wife was shot; troubled to devise some way of seriously damaging or distorting the car's under-carriage after the 'accident.'

Because he gave these factors scant attention and allowed them to betray him, he left 'The Cat' with that first dull gleam of truth – the gold.

When that small banana-shaped piece had dropped from the charred remains of Mrs Elizabeth White, Taylor remembered that gold does not melt until the temperature reaches 1,062 degrees C.

As a scientist, he knew also that if the car had caught fire after overturning it was extremely doubtful that a petrol blaze would have generated sufficient heat to melt a ring to a shapeless mass. He argued that the blaze must have been encouraged manually. The empty petrol tin, he mused, would have explained this away in part. But there must also have been another agency, in all probability a mechanical one.

The crime chemist, who had tinkered with gadgets and engines since he first learned to ride a smoky motor-cycle before the First World War, saw his second gleam of truth when he re-examined the wreckage at the bottom of the culvert.

'This has been a good car,' he had remarked to one of the detectives nearby. 'A Chrysler Plymouth. Oddly enough, it's exactly the same model as the one I drive.'

His colleagues were polite, but their interest was really captured.

'Bit different from other models,' Taylor added. 'Take the petrol tank, for example. It sits lower than the usual type. Turn the car over, and the tank is riding high.'

The seat frame where Raymond White had sat was not burnt as deeply as the frame where his wife had been. The heat had been more intense on her side.

'Well, the rest was easy,' Taylor explained to me. 'When that model of car was overturned, the weight of fuel would exert solid pressure on the opening to the petrol pipe which leads from the tank and runs under the front seat to the carburettor. White was no mug. He was a practical thinker. Make no mistake about that.

'My moment of enlightenment came when it was clear that the petrol feed pipe had been broken just short of that front seat. It was the one break in the line, but it was not an accidental break. It was a deliberate one. White had broken that pipe and bent it to play on the body of his wife after he had shot her carefully through the heart without striking bone, and overturned the car on that precipitous ledge. Then he had ignited the fumes that the weight of petrol in the tank was forcing to the broken end of the pipe. A gallon of petrol was also splashed about liberally to disguise what was going on in the centre of the blaze. Seven inches melted at the broken end of the pipe. The heat ordinarily generated by a car on fire could not have done that.

'Only a murderer who understood the principles of jet or compressed-air torch flames could have known that the infernal arrangement he was creating would generate heat of such intensity that most or all evidence of a diabolical crime should be destroyed. A ship's artificer was the person most likely to have such knowledge. That is why, days earlier, I was convinced that the man we sought probably had had experience at sea, and undoubtedly in the engine-room of a warship.

'It must have taken White a few minutes to get things working. That is why the detectives re-checked his timings. White was always so very certain of the time the "tragedy" occurred. He had seen the clock at the Hunt farmhouse, he said. Yet the farmers insisted – never knowing why this seemingly innocent point was checked so thoroughly – that their only clock was in a room White had never entered.'

Former artificer Farrell, so near success in crime again, went to his death still hoping that his guilt and scheming would never be exposed so blatantly. His last note, found near his body, read: 'Please don't blame anyone for this. I've lost my dear wife. I want to be with her and I cannot live without her.'

But the coroner was not impressed. In fact, he was incensed, realising that, as all three principals of the drawn-out drama were dead, he could only record an open verdict.

Bluntly he told the court he would not believe White's story.

And then – whether justified or not may be debatable – he flayed those who made the first inquiries the night the car was burning.

'It was most unfortunate that the body of the deceased was not taken from under the car at the earliest possible moment,' he said. 'It was left unguarded for several hours during the night of her death. I am of the opinion that the facts and circumstances surrounding this death should have been examined with greater care immediately after the occurrence.'

The coroner realised that only because the full horror of the death had not been readily apparent White had been allowed the delayed-time advantage which so often is vital in a mystery probe. Which reflects even greater credit on the experts later called on to unravel an amazing tangle of doubts, rumours, lies, questionable coincidences and, finally, unassailable facts.

3 Arsenic and Old Bricks

We can talk of ships, shoes and sealing-wax as we peer through Taylor's microscope of memories for the first time. Or of aircraft, bricks and parrots for that matter, or almost anything you care to name that could figure in crime or mystery as gripping as the best of Edgar Wallace.

Taylor's own appetite for mystery before his retirement was sharp and never fully satisfied. His knowledge is prodigious. From effect he tracked back relentlessly and logically to cause. From cause he sought motive. And if motive was not clear he was often able to unlock secrets that lay buried in another altogether different age.

* * *

Victoria was a colourful, cosmopolitan and lusty colony when Charles Anthony Taylor was born in it in 1885. By cable, by camel, by courier or cart, the discovery of fabulous amounts of gold had been flashed years before to the Cornish miners under the English Channel, to the rice paddies of inland China, and to the goldfields of Alaska.

A vast area of central Victoria had been covered by the drills, spades, picks and bare hands of some hundred thousand miners who had surged into the colony with dreams of wealth. From Maryborough to Bendigo, to Castlemaine and Kyneton, the rattle of the pans around the clock was as consistent as the jingle of the Cobb and Company harness on the horses opening up the Pony Express-like shuttle service to the roaring diggings.

More than fifty thousand Chinese had flocked to the diggings by 1888. Many who became richer through the quest returned to their homeland to obey its ancient call of '*Lok yip gway gun.*' 'When the leaves fall, truly they must return to the roots.' More stayed to exhaust their optimism by fossicking on the fields, and a number converged on Bohemian Melbourne.

Melbourne's Chinatown, at the east end of the city, was being ruled – as were the Chinese settlements on the diggings – by a sinister secret society, the powerful Gee Hing tong. I believe it still exists in a quite peaceful form today. But in the twilight of the gold rush age it was still under grave suspicion for the baffling and still unsolved disappearance of Constable Ryan at the Bendigo goldfields in 1886.

I include these facts partly to outline some idea of the living climate of those times. It was one of the most exotic chapters in Australian history.

As it passed, the main bodies of miners drifted away. They left only small rearguards of optimists and contrivers to grub for leftovers among the stark and ugly slag and mullock heaps. With billy tea and flour-and-water damper baked in coals as their staple diet, they lived in crude shelters of iron slabs and gum or wattle bark. They shaped clay bricks with calloused hands to make small kilns for smelting down their last hope – 'fool's gold.'

But eventually the great minefields were deserted. Their rich history of endeavour and thwarted hopes, of wildest dreams unfulfilled, of riots, hatred, lawlessness, rebellion and insoluble comradeship – these were little more than memories when the boy Taylor played outside the old mining township of Maryborough around 1895.

But they were memories with echoes that would ring vibrantly through some of his sternest tasks ahead. And never more so than in the burning summer heat of 1925 when far north bush police sent out a murder call.

A young and pretty woman teacher at a country school was dead. Several of a family with whom she had been boarding had been vomiting wretchedly and been gravely ill. The cause was uncertain, but poison was suspected. The killer was unknown. So was the motive.

Taylor's wife – a small, cheerful and attentive woman – remembered the morning nearly forty years ago when her husband was given these meagre facts by a messenger at the door.

'Charlie just threw a few things in a leather bag and left as though he were off to his lab. as usual,' she recalled. 'Just a couple of shirts and handkerchiefs and a magnifying glass. He was never one for carrying a lot of instruments, you know. His chief equipment was his head.'

Taylor told me he was still thinking aloud three hours after he arrived at the timber, bark and sheet-iron vineyard houses about twelve miles outside Nyah West. He was hot and tired after a boring, 230-mile journey by slow steam train from Melbourne to the far north-west grape-growing district on the border of New South Wales.

His suit – 'the three-piece ash tray' it was often called – was rumpled and clung to him in the heat. His hair, with the first dash of iron-grey at the temples, was teased out near his ears like that of a koala bear.

He toyed with a scone and a piece of currant cake as he sank into the shade of a great redgum. He mopped the perspiration off his thin rimmed spectacles and blinked through the haze bouncing off the dry plains that sprawled to the Murray River.

Taylor nibbled at the cake again. Then he spat it out. There was no doubt, he decided, that there was arsenic in this food. And that cold tea in the pot at the farmhouse kitchen was almost loaded with it. In fact, its density would be consistent with the quantity that would have been needed to cause the young schoolteacher's agonising and violent death. Further, it was in proportion to the poison found in her stomach during the autopsy just made in Melbourne by the Government pathologist, Dr Crawford Mollison.

It appeared that the police were right. Despite an apparent lack of clear motive, someone among the few orchardists and vignerons in or near this sun-baked homestead had deliberately planted lethal doses in the food and teapot, knowing that the average Australian schoolmistress would never go without her cup of tea.

He was confident that the murderer would be found outside

the homestead, because, if this was murder, it was a pretty clumsy case. The killer was more likely to be someone in the district who knew the habits of this grape-grower's family and their schoolteacher boarder.

Taylor had spoken to everyone who had been at the homestead. He knew that it had been bandied about that the villain was the vigneron. In fact, this was the unshakable opinion of more than one experienced policeman.

The farmer himself had not been well for months. The heat of early summer had got him down, or so he said. He had spent a lazy vacation in the south and returned, much more vigorous and cheerful, to supervise the bumper harvesting of grapes. Then suddenly, while he was feeling better, the girl teacher boarding with him died. And he and others on the farm had simultaneously been taken ill.

The characters of this farmer's family and their friends were unimpeachable, and there was not one trace of poison on the farm. Taylor had searched the homestead painstakingly for hours. There wasn't one medicine bottle in the place. Further, he was sure that even if ten men and tidy women had tried to eradicate all evidence of having had poison on that farm, he would have found evidence of it.

Now, the farmer had a healthy family, mentally and physically. They were normal, extrovert country folk. None was a hypochondriac. None showed a trace of psychopathic tendencies, deep-seated grudges, carefully hidden phobias or had anything to gain by murder.

Taylor mopped his face and spectacles again. He recalls formulating some questions.

For instance, was the farmer's earlier illness also the result of an unsuccessful attempt to murder him? Had that same intending killer been more successful when he later laid the same bait for the schoolmistress? Was it, after all, the farmer who should be unmasked? What could he be anxious to conceal? Or was there an astounding challenge here, another sort of riddle with a mocking clue he could not see?

'I became really lost in thought as the sun was going down that day,' Taylor told me at his home. 'It was sinking below the fringe of gums before I stirred. I stuffed that nibbled cake in my pocket and walked back thoughtfully through the cooling evening. I could easily have been sure this was a case of heavy-fisted outback murder, except for one small thing. My experience of cooking was limited enough, but I had been a food analyst, and I knew enough about ingredients to ask myself why was the arsenic so strong in some places, moderately strong in others, and in others entirely lacking?'

He had the nagging feeling of standing on the threshold of something very strange. Here were the many symptoms of a projected mass murder, and yet his brain rejected them.

He found that the back was the coolest part of the homestead as the shadows lengthened. There was a small white seat beside a well, and he sat on it. It was a soft twilight, one that would end in 'the lustrous purple blackness of the soft Australian night.' A gentle breeze sprang up and a few leaves withered by heat and lack of rain scurried across the dust and fluttered down the well.

'How difficult it is to evaluate in words the moment when a harmless trifle suddenly blossoms into shattering significance,' Taylor recalled that day I visited him. 'I remember that scores of ordinary dried and brittle gum and acacia leaves were scuttling around me when the breeze sprang up. My eyes followed a few. They fell into the shadows of the well and fluttered to the water about ten feet below. I suppose my eyes tracked them because they were spinning down spirally and gracefully. I remember seeing a brief flash of reflected light as they disturbed the cool water surface.'

The last quivers of reflected twilight on the water vanished. But Taylor, standing by the well, saw two pale patches down there on the surface. He gripped the edge of the seven-foot-wide well and peered down closer.

Those two pale, phosphorescent scraps down there were not leaves or bits of paper. They were dead frogs. He could see their white upturned bellies. They were frogs that had grown to maturity in the well, the coolest part of the whole farm, and should not have died. Why had they? The answer was in that well – because there was arsenic in its water. It had killed those frogs.

There was also arsenic in the tea, which had been brewed

from that well water before the police had ordered the farmer and his family to disturb nothing on the premises. Arsenic was in the cake he had eaten, too, and in soup and other foods in which only well water had been used as a mixing or a thinning fluid.

Moreover, he had found no trace of arsenic in scones and other food in which milk had been used instead of water.

Taylor pulled out his hand magnifying glass and, by torch-light now, closely examined all the inside top bricks around the parapet of the well. He observed that they were hand-made bricks, well-shaped and sound. Arsenic had been put into that well quite recently in density sufficient to kill a young school-teacher, apart from the two big frogs. So there should be traces of arsenic's fine white powder somewhere on the bricks.

He could find none, but the next morning he proved conclusively that the water in the well – a good five feet of it – was heavily impregnated with the poison.

That day life returned to the homestead and the vineyards, which had been silent and deserted for a day or two. The last of the fat grapes had been picked and were to be washed and dried before crating and despatch as raisins and sultanas. The seasonal work had been resumed on the understanding that the homestead should not be entered and the water in the well not be drunk.

About 10 a.m. 'The Cat' was pondering by the mystery well again when two workmen innocently but dramatically interrupted his thoughts. They were carrying buckets and kerosene cans cut down to half their original height. All had holes punched in the bottoms, and were filled with grapes. 'The Cat's' eyes narrowed as he watched the labourers from the vineyard prepare to lower the buckets and tins into the well so that the water would sluice over the grapes for the last time before they dried.

This was the tiny but amazing clue his restless mind had sought.

'Hold it!' he commanded. 'Haven't you been told this water must not be used?'

That wasn't quite the order, the labourers said. They had been told not to drink it. They had always come to the well to rinse the grapes.

Taylor ran his fingers around the lips of the buckets and tins. He tasted the moisture there. He smelt the buckets, and then he asked questions that took the cheerful workmen by surprise.

All the time they had been working on the place, they said, they'd always used potash or a very mild solution of caustic for rinsing the grapes when they were picked. It was the last process before washing them again in the well water and setting them out to dry. Took the wax or something off the grapes.

Taylor was well aware of that. It was a natural wax. More properly, it was a bloom. He had learned that at Geelong's Gordon Institute not so long before, and then through those fascinating 'Promote Mildura and its Products' days.

He was, in short, a fruit expert. But he was a mines and minerals expert, too.

'These tins of yours,' he said to the workmen. 'You have just used them for sluicing these grapes through the potash or caustic troughs over there to remove the bloom from them?'

'That's right,' the workmen said. 'We've been doing this since the season started. It's the regular routine.'

'Exactly,' said 'The Cat.' 'But the tins had a little drop of potash or caustic on them when they went down the well the first time?'

The workmen admitted this could be the case.

Taylor smiled at them. The end was in sight. Everything would be all right, he assured the anxious labourers. There was nothing to worry about. The few drops on the tin would not hurt anyone.

There was only one point to be cleared up, and only the farmer could provide the answer.

'Let's go back over events,' Taylor invited him. 'The bricks of the well are hand-made, but you did not make them. You built this well about a year ago. About two months later – that is, some ten months ago – you suddenly became ill when you were here on your own for a time, and then went south for a holiday. Those upsets of yours began after last year's harvest. Do you remember exactly when and where you got those bricks?'

The farmer packed his pipe and told him: 'You know, there's been a terrific shortage of bricks since the war ended. I went all the way to Bendigo for these – about eighty miles. I bought them cheap from a cove who had been dismantling the old disused chimney-stacks on the deserted goldfields. I brought them back with my horse and cart.'

'The Cat' nodded. 'I thought as much,' he smiled. 'It's just as well I noticed they were hand-made bricks. Now, excuse me while I potter around.'

He carried his search to the bottom of the well. There, on the lower bricks, he found the heavy deposits of arsenic he had been seeking.

It was murder? No.

Negligence? Not really.

Could it have been a chance in a million? In fact, it was a chance in a hundred million!

'The Cat' made his report to the Government.

'Years ago,' he wrote, 'after the fever of the gold rush, only a handful of prospectors were left on the diggings at Bendigo and other places. Some fossicked and panned for specks of gold. Others discovered "fool's gold," which has some of the appearance, but none of the worth, of true gold. Science knows it as arseno-pyrites.

'So that this pyrites could be burned and its few marketable products thus be withdrawn, some of the last prospectors made bricks with their hands and built chimney or furnace stacks. In this process, arsenic was given off in a kind of smoke. A lot of it was always deposited on the bricks inside the flue. If a normal fire were being used, most of the poison would be trapped in the lower bricks. If the fire were hotter than usual arsenic smoke would be taken towards the top and deposited there. The height of the arsenic deposit's level would, therefore, be somewhat in ratio to the temperature of the fire and the draught.

'Nearly all the fires had been of average heat. On my homeward journey from Nyah West I went to the old goldfields at Bendigo, found the dealer who had sold the bricks, and established that they had been taken from a kiln where the temperature had been normal and constant – that is, most of the arsenic had been trapped in bricks near the bottom of the dismantled kiln. When this kiln was dismantled the dealer washed the bricks. They appeared clean, and he would have no knowledge that arsenic was trapped inside. The bricks were then loaded on to the farmer's cart in the order in which they had been dismantled. Bricks from the top – holding little or no arsenic – were loaded first. The lower bricks – still holding powerful doses of arsenic even after about half a century – were loaded last. These, of course, were first to be unloaded up at the Nyah West vineyard and went to the bottom of the pile. So, the bricks which so long ago had absorbed most arsenic became the top of the well, and those bricks containing least arsenic the bottom of the well.

'But this is by no means the solution to the mystery although the key is near.

'Arsenic is slightly soluble in water. So a slow process of solution did begin when drinking water was put into the well. Soon afterwards the farmer and others became strangely ill. The farmer was affected most because he was there most of the time. It was not the climate that disagreed with him, as he had thought. It was the contaminated water, which did not yet contain enough arsenic to kill him, and which, under normal conditions, may not have reached that concentration for some years. But he would have known none of that when he went south. When he returned, naturally he felt improved. The pretty young schoolteacher arrived to board with him during her posting to the local school headed by a Mr James Sutcliffe.

'The well then was almost dry after a serious drought. But a few days later, as grape harvest time came round again, a summer storm broke and the water level of the well soon rose. For the first time since it had been built it began to lap the old kiln bricks.

'The seasonal workers who had returned to the district to pick and wash the grapes again were pleased to find a convenient well had been built since they were there before. On the day the big grape-washing began someone drew water from the well for baking a cake, and to make tea for the young teacher. But by then a tragic clash of extremely rare, if not unique, coincidences had taken place. Not long before the teacher's water had been drawn, the first grape-washing bucket had been lowered in the well. It still held slight traces of potash. Normally these would have been harmless in that much water. But a violent chemical convulsion took place in that well. The arsenic that had been locked in those top hand-made bricks since the last century was released into the water in deadly strength.

'Nothing can unlock arsenic so instantly as that mild solution the farmer had used to ensure that his grapes were clean and wholesome for the market! The first plunge of the bucket was the eerie stroke of death. The well bricks near the top released a flood of the poison that also snuffed out the life of the healthy frogs. This was a case where commendable attention to hygiene led, by extraordinary reactions, to one of the most unusual mysteries in our files.'

Melbourne Herald

'The Cat' at work

This drawing of Alma Tirtschke was made with relatives' co-operation soon after her murder

Colin Ross at the time of his trial

Bourke Street, Melbourne, in 1921. Alma Tirtschke's body was found in Gun Alley, off Little Collins Street, just over 100 yards behind their frontage

The Whites' farmhouse outside Walwa

Raymond White's overturned car in the culvert off the Jingellic Road.
Police cars in the background

George Green under arrest for the murders of Annie and Phyllis Wiseman

Dr. Crawford Mollison

Bristol Beaufort over Australia. An official RAAF photograph of the plane which crashed in alarming numbers

Arnold Karl Sodeman, strangler of four girls, after his arrest

Edward John Leonski at police headquar

The recess at Albert Park where Ivy McLeod was murdered

The apartment steps in Spring Street where Pauline Thompson was murdered

'The Mad Yank', in the exercise yard of the Melbourne city watch-house, awaits execution

In his cell Leonski produced many sketches. He sent this one to his defence counsel

An Aborigine blacktracker and Senior-Constable Haygarth examine footprints in the Royal Park slit trench where Gladys Hosking was slain

Detectives Adam and Mooney arrive with exhibits at the Leonski court-martial

4 Through Australia's Gravest Hour

SOMEWHERE along the Thames in the early winter of 1942 dockers with the speedy prosecution of the war at heart believed they had one more cause for rejoicing. Rommel was on the run. Montgomery was a new star in the war-shaken firmament. Bombs were falling on Berlin, and the dockers had just battened down the hatches on what they rightly assumed was the first urgent consignment of sleek new Spitfires for Australia to throw against the Japanese. There were several dozen crates, each about twenty feet by ten feet by nine feet, and each held a complete aircraft modified for heat, dust and moisture conditions along the North Australian fringe.

Only a few persons had been told officially and exactly what the crates contained and why and where they were required without delay. But obviously some hint of the vessel's urgent mission must have leaked at least some days before to an enemy mastermind whose plans to cripple Australian defences would soon be foiled almost twelve thousand miles away by Australia's greatest crime chemist.

The ship cleared the Thames and Channel, and as the known U-boat threat receded it seemed that the voyage – historic for Australia and the American Cavalry Division and other fighting men being rushed out to her aid – might be tense but uneventful for those aboard.

It was – until that fourth day at sea, when a fierce fire broke out in the hold.

It was not a common blaze. It was frighteningly savage for

its size. None of the seamen ordered to the hold had experienced such heat before, or had had to battle desperately with a blaze for so long with little more than hoses, fire extinguishers and sand. It was the type of fire that required special appliances for encircling and killing it at its place of origin, and it was only by the concerted determination of an exhausted crew that the blaze was quenched.

There were no similar incidents on board. The ship kept strict radio silence about the fire, and inflexibly she kept on a predetermined course. The captain was silent until the fine morning when, arousing no attention from a war-time Melbourne long accustomed to all manner of ships from battlewagons to salt-caked 'sweepers, she hove to in Port Phillip Bay.

Only the captain went ashore. When he returned alone the ship moved into dock. Cables were thrown aboard. Shore leave was cancelled. The ship was left in the isolation of a top-level quarantine. Then the telephones hummed between the ship and shore, and between the offices of the Air Staff at the ivy-clad Victoria Barracks and the offices of the other war emergency service headquarters in the city.

One of the few to be taken into immediate and strictest confidence at Victoria Barracks was Squadron-Leader E. W. Rosewarne. He was one of three policemen – the others were Wing-Commander C. V. Ashe, M.C., and Squadron-Leader Ted North, M.V.O. – who had been seconded for special services for the duration.

'At the time this ship crept in I was a liaison officer between the RAAF security service and the RAAF Provost Corps,' Rosewarne said later. 'I was brought into the inquiry immediately because there were grave reasons to believe it was a top security matter.

'I was summoned from my office to a nearby room. Already there were the group-captain in charge of RAAF Intelligence, and Mr Justice George Augustus Pape, a Supreme Court judge serving, like myself, for the duration. There I heard the first few bald facts known and was told to take over the RAAF interests in the case.

'These preliminaries indicated only that one Spitfire had been completely destroyed by a fire of incredible power and speed, which may have damaged others required so badly in the north while bombers from Timor were still hammering the coast.'

Were there any signs of carelessness? Rosewarne asked. No one knew, but that was highly problematical.

Could this have been an accident? There was no evidence to suggest as much.

Was there something strangely combustible in the hold? Nothing of a foreign or peculiar nature was known to the master and his crew.

Was it sabotage? No actual evidence was to hand. But the fire had been so fierce that all other aircraft and the whole ship had been in greatest peril. It was considered opinion that, unless the cause of the fire was established quickly, none of the other urgent consignments might reach Australia. The ship's officers had ensured that the remains of the fighter and its crate had not been disturbed. They had been inspected initially at a distance of several feet, and there was no visible sign of a fire having started outside the crate.

Sworn to secrecy, three other men were called in on the case. They were the Chief Fire Officer, Mr James Kemp, his successor Mr L. P. Whitehead, and the Government Analyst, Charles Anthony Taylor.

Rosewarne had declared that one of the tightest security nets of the war was drawn around the investigation by experts.

'In fact, it never has been lifted,' he added recently. 'Until now I have never mentioned it, nor heard it mentioned elsewhere for more than twenty years. Like the Beaufort mystery that I attended later, this was one of the most hush-hush periods while Australia was at war. The real man of the hour was that remarkable old chap, Charles Taylor. He had the all-seeing eye.'

Now, for the first time, it is possible to follow that eye's gaze into a wartime top-secret mystery.

The charred crate and gutted aircraft were unloaded at an isolated wharf.

'The remains were trucked to Laverton aerodrome, fourteen miles from Melbourne, by RAAF transport,' Rosewarne told me. 'I drove Taylor to the scene, and we found armed guards from the RAAF Service Police posted around a hangar as the ashes and other black remains were spread carefully over probably five hundred square yards of concrete.'

Most of the crate was cinders. But at some points inside the fire had almost eaten through the remaining planks as it was engulfing the machine. Substantial areas of the timber were found to be only paper-thick. The tough metal at the rubbled end of the crate had been subjected to heat so intense that it had melted and then hardened into incongruous shapes. That was the first significant point in 'The Cat's' analysis, but he did not say so at the time.

He proceeded to make a minute inspection of every part that could be salvaged from the wreck. For two days technicians sieved every ember, strand of wire and piece of twisted tube through sheets of small-mesh chicken wire. But there were no detectable remains of impregnated swabs, of fuel, spirit or tins of a size that could have been deliberately or carelessly thrust inside the crate.

For a time it looked like a hopeless quest. But after many hours small but undeniable characteristics of that fire were observed that would have escaped a layman's attention. These fine points rammed home the conviction that the enemy had been unusually active between the Spitfire factory and the Pool of London – or else at sea. It was 5 p.m. when the team's efforts yielded the first glimmer of reward. At the bottom of a sieve they found a harmless-looking piece of metal. It was smaller than a thumb, and had been twisted by heat and partly melted. Like almost every other part, it was badly stained.

Taylor, Rosewarne, Kemp, Whitehead and the professional Service officers did not feel inclined to admit that it was significant, and yet it did appear to be the one small part, despite its twisted form, for which the aircraft specialists could not conclusively account.

'The Cat' wrapped it in his handkerchief and dropped it in his pocket. It was unwrapped that night on the desk of his museum-like laboratory. He worked late and undisturbed, sipping coffee from a beaker on a Bunsen burner, and munching celery sandwiches brought from a kiosk down the street. By dawn he knew without any doubt that Australia's desperately needed Spitfires and those to follow – which 'Bluey' Truscott and his men back home from the Battle of Britain should fly – were never intended to arrive.

As the sun rose and he marshalled his salient points in logical order, Taylor again had the glowing satisfaction of knowing the answer to one of the best-kept secrets of the Pacific war.

Twenty years after that memorable morning when he had started the report that was to stagger Whitehall, he began his flashback story for me with talk about wood, brown coal, briquettes and similar fuel that one would burn in a large domestic fireplace. A roaring fire like that might generate heat up to some 700 degrees F., he said. It would make iron or steel red-hot.

But, as his wartime report had pointed out, if an ordinary fire, deliberate or accidental, had started outside the Spitfire crates, it could not have melted any of the metal of the aircraft packed inside. Nor could it have swept from the outside to the inside of the crate and then turned round and eaten away the walls, because it was quite clear to the experts at the Laverton hangar that the inside of the planking surface had burned first.

Therefore the fire had been started, somehow, inside the heavy steel-bound crate. The vital question was why had this happened suddenly after several uneventful days at sea?

As Taylor worked on his report, he turned to that challenging little piece of distorted metal again. It was only a fraction more than half an inch across. Originally it apparently belonged to a unit that might have been about three inches long – no more. There were signs that it may have been one of two parts which had screwed together like a fountain pen to its top.

Very fine parallel lines were found by Taylor at one spot on this metal. They covered an area no larger than a piece of confetti. But they fascinated Taylor when he peered at them through his magnifying glass because he knew they were only part of a complete band of them that once had gone right round a small cylinder.

They were the finest threads he remembered having seen, milled to a thousandth of an inch. This was watchmaker's precision, he wrote. More significantly, their pitch was neither British nor American. It had the hallmark of the joint work of a German scientist teamed up with a meticulous engineer.

Taylor then noticed that the mangled part he held was made from a type of brass. This was important because the thirty or so different types of brass, right up to hard bell metal, are resistant to acid. Taylor concluded that whoever made the cylinder certainly knew his brass!

Next he concentrated on a few tiny stains at one end of this evidence. They showed that an acid had been there, for they were stains of copper sulphate, which pointed to sulphuric acid being present. Sulphuric acid in touch with copper would produce copper sulphate.

So copper also had been there!

'The Cat' knew he was holding the remains of a perfect time bomb. It was one so small that it could be hidden in the instep of a shoe, and yet so lethal that, given a few seconds' start, it could generate a fire that would eat out the body of a sturdy ship. As far as he knew, it was the most powerful time bomb ever known in Australia.

Taylor completed his report on his findings, which was delivered to a grave RAAF officer at his office for immediate despatch to Whitehall. And it was that report, secret until now, that ended sabotage of this sort.

'The exhibit had been part of an innocent-looking cylinder of small proportions,' he said. 'But it was a Tom Thumb bomb of extraordinary ferocity. It could have been only the joint creation of scientists and engineers with great resources and an intelligent organisation behind them. This enemy group must have thoroughly understood the principles of delayed incendiaries and had remarkable machinists to fashion the materials.

'The cylinder had two divisions. These were separated crossways by a disc of copper so that one half of the cylinder was cut off from the other. In the upper half of this cylinder was highly concentrated sulphuric acid. It was as water-free and concentrated as this acid can be made. In the lower half was a mere thimbleful of potassium chlorate. There was not a chance in a million that the cylinder could leak.

'This complete cylinder was quite harmless while the chemicals remained in their own compartments. But the thickness of that dividing copper disc had been calculated to ensure that the sulphuric acid could not eat through it for, say, three to four days. By this time, a ship usually would be well at sea and probably off coasts that were not friendly.

'Immediately the two chemical components came into contact a tremendous amount of oxygen was generated and liberated. Simultaneously there was a brilliant flash of spontaneous combustion flame. There was no really frightening explosion to give warning – only a large and unusual puff as the vivid flame appeared to rise from nothing. But an extraordinary chain reaction set in immediately. The devouring flame was boosted by the oxygen the phial of chemicals itself was creating. In turn, this increasing flame was fed by oxygen in the air. It was a process of repetition that went on and on, multiplying all the time.

'That spreading flame generated heat of much more than 1,000 degrees F., the minimum temperature required to have ensured the melting and twisting of the metal components of the destroyed aircraft. It was providential to our cause that the fire was seen very soon after it began. The precious cargo could have been saved only by the most prompt and brave attention to the blaze; because there was enough fury in that tiny phial to have destroyed a six-room house in half an hour.'

* * *

Bright and fair was the morning when H.M. Australian corvette *Castlemaine* crept past the bomb-blasted wrecks of the *Neptunia, Zealandia, Meggs* and other once-stout ships in Darwin harbour. She had crossed the Timor Sea without air or submarine alerts carrying sick men who limped and scrambled ashore after months pinning down the Japanese at Timor air bases until Spitfires reached Australia. A medical major met the commandos on the wharf and guided them to trucks and cars to go to the clean, cool white Karlon Hospital with the red cross on the roof. 'Eat, relax, and let us see what we can do for you,' he said, 'until movements can be fixed to send you south.'

Men sick and wounded and repatriated secretly from the

Timor struggle found it good to see the signal station on the cliff again, the shambles that once was Darwin's Chinatown, the deserted bloodhouse pubs with the drooping, squeaking, swinging doors, the ruins of the two original main streets – 'one for whites and the other for bloody poor whites' – the big fuel tanks, not bleeding, smoking and crumpling now, and the screen of the one open-air theatre where *Darktown Strutters' Ball* and *In Town Tonight* had been battered from the tinny piano while the wary talons of searchlights had clawed nervously at the sky's black throat.

So much was familiar, and yet the air was charged with change. Somehow a great confidence could be sensed at this back door of the nation under arms.

Once there had been tension and strain, and the acceptance that, if the enemy did come cascading down the tropical Daly and Roper Rivers in bamboo-raft armadas, one might have to fight with almost empty hands.

But now the seamen were sprightly and the commodores good-humouredly urbane. The sloop *Platypus*, whose wailing siren at midday had warned of approaching bombers from Timor, had not sounded off for days. Truck convoys were travelling south and north on time. The hurriedly called-up toilers of the Civil Construction Corps were sun-bronzed and hardened now, and hewing trails out through the pampas and pandanus palms, and the spinifex and stunted gums of a timeless land. The blacks were returning from 'alonga fella bush.' Sometimes glasses tinkled merrily in messes which not long before could not afford a famished and wandering soldier a crust of bread or a four-ounce tin of bully beef.

The reasons were soon seen. They streaked in from the sea.

'The Spitfire boys,' the major explained.

He said it comfortably, like a man sipping dream-like brandy after food fit for the gods. Moreover, he had the expression of a man who might have added: 'We're glad they're here, and we hope they never go.'

What he did add was: 'They've just come up from south, you know. Just a few, but they've turned the tide. We were scared they'd never come. And somehow, you know, we feel they reached us just in time.'

5 Quite a Bright Bird!

THE quaint puzzle of the few big pigs, which was brought gravely to the notice of H.M. Minister for Agriculture, a very tall and most distinguished-looking person, did not involve loss of human life. But to those few who know and appreciate the story, it ranks with the mystery of Arsenic and Old Bricks as an admirable example of deduction and of common-sense investigation leading back most shrewdly from the ultimate effect to the invisible but undeniable cause.

It may seem droll for top Crown men to explore the many ways by which pigs die, especially as one will never know precisely which factor suddenly boosted the inquiry from a local case to a high-level political probe.

Perhaps the pigs' owner had suitable political influence or a credit for services to be met. Probably the atmosphere at the time was more generally charged with fear of sabotage than is imagined today. Certainly the minister of the day, in concord with his party colleagues, tenderly nursed every single vote in shaky country zones; and it must be recognised that, in any Australian town, a threat against a farmer's stock is aggression against the man himself, particularly when the fear spreads that poison or epidemic may be abroad.

Whatever the prime reason, Taylor recalled clearly that the case was hoisted to priority early in 1940 when Mr Ned Hogan – a former State Premier, and then Minister for Agriculture – presented police headquarters and the Health Department with a curt Governmental directive for expert attention without delay.

One hot morning in February of that year a woman farming at lovely Yarra Glen, thirty-two miles from Melbourne, told the local police she was sure she had heard a car stop near her expensive model piggeries during the night, and it was unusual for cars to stop on that lonely stretch of the highway after dark. Whether she had imagined the sound of the car or not, there seemed to be something sinister and mysterious in the incident because she found that one of her most valuable prize pigs had died suddenly.

A few days later another monster porker died. Then another. The local police believed all had been poisoned. But veterinary surgeons who assisted them admitted they were mystified.

'At this stage the Government kicked up sheer hell,' Taylor told me, chuckling as he recalled the case. 'The word went round that anything could happen in wartime and that this case warranted the attention of the Government Analyst's Department. Detectives from Camberwell CIB, with other problems bigger even than the pigs, were ordered to drive me to the farm. It was near the highway, but off a rough bush track. About thirty paces to the right of the farmhouse were the pig pens, enclosed by a post-and-rail fence about twenty yards square.

'The countryside was undulating, with a few grass-clad knolls sticking up here and there. There were several clumps of trees a few hundred yards away, and many others in the distance. They were not tall trees. Some were rather scrawny. By far the biggest were three majestic ironbark gums, spreading branches over the pens to give the pigs shade from heat and shelter from rain. The pens had been put at that spot because the next clump of trees was about a quarter of a mile away and comprised pretty miserable specimens of the Australian gum.'

Taylor said the woman was still 'hopping mad' about losing her pigs and dreading the loss of all, and that she unreservedly gave opinions about the action she expected.

'She couldn't get that car from her mind,' he went on. 'She kept talking about thieves in the night and killers who must be gaoled. But, personally, I felt she was a bit up a tree herself on the subject of that car, and had imagined it.'

Taylor explained how he lit a cigarette as he sauntered off alone to look at the rolling green countryside and pause occasionally to pluck and appreciate the small wildflowers peeping demurely from the grass. While several farmers idly chewed straws and sceptically watched his seemingly peculiar movements, he tramped for almost half a mile around the pens.

He swept a keen eye over the contours of the landscape, speculated about the depth of loam, the lower formations, and even the probable yield compared to acres nearer the river flats. He sat down on a hillock, and lit a fresh cigarette. Away in the distance the remaining pigs were grunting and his cynical audience snorting.

Taylor has always loved the good rich earth. He loved the orchids and bush flowers he had gathered as a boy, loved to feel earth trickle through his short, strong fingers, and loved to wonder how the sun's rays could bring the green in grass to life. Emerald green, like those thick long blades at the base of this lonely hill. And lighter greens, like that patch farther up the slope.

As he mused Taylor scratched slowly at the crust of the crest with a broken twig. Yes, it was poorer earth up here. That would account for the inferior colour and grade of grass. Probably this was an outcrop of some sort. There were numbers in the locality, and they were seldom a blessing to the farmers.

Suddenly he rose and kicked off a divot with the sharp edge of his heel. He scratched the harder surface again and picked up a handful of the soil.

He was still shaking it in his palm as he wandered back to the bored and silent group around the pens. He thinks five minutes passed before he spoke. He looked at the pigs and the pens, and he peered at the bright blue sky.

He said to the woman: 'The animals you lost, they were really big?'

'I'll say they were!' the woman retorted. 'Very valuable sows. None better in Australia. Worth a small fortune to us, too. I can't afford to lose my other pigs, and I'm in plenty of trouble as it is.'

Taylor picked something up from the dust and thrust it in his pocket. Then, as he returned to his waiting car, he allowed himself another of his deep-throated chuckles.

One farmer nudged his neighbour as the analyst passed.

'Hey!' he said. 'Did you see? Catch on to what that cove picked up?'

'Uh-huh!' the other said. 'We've some funny coots about.'

* * *

Under a powerful hooded lamp at his laboratory, 'The Cat' looked closely at a few small black crystals he had spread on his blotting pad. They were like black tea leaves that had been allowed to dry and set quite hard. He reached out for an unglazed porcelain jar.

With tweezers, he stroked the black crystals along the side of the jar, using a regular sweeping motion. As he had expected, the crystals left a brown streak along the jar. They had scratched into the unglazed porcelain surface like a nail file.

He poured the black crystals into a test-tube. They dropped to the bottom in a black layer about one and a half inches across and one-eighth of an inch deep. He dissolved the crystals, shook the tube, added calculated amounts of chemicals, and finally was left with a transformation – white salts, and others of a pretty orange shade.

He took a strange exhibit from the pocket of his grey twill suit. It was a small dead bird, with brilliant red feathers, others that were a true yellow and a vivid green. The bird was a Rosella parrot, one of the flocks to be found in the Yarra Glen and other districts – the specimen he had snatched up quickly from the dust outside the pen.

He picked up a scalpel, one of several he had preserved from the time, long before, when he had abandoned medicine to obey the call of physical science. On the desk top he made a neat post-mortem of the bird, sure he had been right, that, while sitting on the mound and soaking in the hot sunshine, he had unlocked a mystery of the years.

He scraped some of the contents of the tiny stomach into another test-tube, and after he had treated it like the first by adding the same chemicals he was left with those white salts again. And, also, those pretty orange salts. This meant that the contents of the bird's stomach were exactly the same as the black crystals he had taken from his stock and dissolved in the unglazed porcelain jar.

He had solved a curious mystery because he had thought it important to concentrate on the sex of the pigs that died, to study and interpret the landscape of that farm, to remember that pigs don't fly, but Rosella parrots do.

Taylor drafted the following illuminating report:

'To the Hon. the Minister for Agriculture.

'I noticed first that the trees in the district were many years old yet growing, mainly, in rather scrawny and patchy clumps. There was one great clearing, about four hundred yards wide, where there was no sign of a tree. But I was impressed by the four great specimens of ironbark gum that presided over the pens, which spread great branches over the pigs to offer shade.

'The pigs I saw were in prime condition. Their surroundings were excellent. Their water was pure and there was no chance that any animal had been affected by exposure. There was no visible trace of any poison an intruder could have thrown to them.

'As I browsed around, I noticed that one hillock appeared to be out of harmony with the surrounding landscape. It was my impression that it did not appear to fit in naturally with the apparent contours and soil layers of the land. The grass on this crest and around it was weaker and paler than that around its base – this often being a pointer to soil deficiency. I scraped away part of this crest surface. It was quite hard. I clutched from it a small handful of dust, stones and other material which obviously had flaked off somehow horizontally from longer, needle-like formations. This "other material" was in the form of small black crystals.

'I suspected then, because there were scratchings here and there, that Rosella parrots, throughout a century-old quest for shellgrit, gravel, or similar roughage which they must have, had worked away at the surface of this hillock and found that these small black crystals were ideal for their purpose. Satisfied, they had then flown away.

'Sometimes they had perched on the branches of the only giant ironbark gums in sight, those around or above the big pens, because Rosella parrots must perch high. They did not favour those smaller and lower trees around the countryside, which obviously were scrawnier because of some soil deficiency. I knew that some of the birds had perched on limbs directly above those pens. Others, such as a bird I have dissected, must have perched on limbs that spread outside the railing limits of the pens. In the stomach of this dissected bird I found small black crystals.

'Porcleain and chemical tests reduced the black crystals to white and orange salts. These established that the black crystals were stibnite.

'Stibnite is first cousin to antimony, which is a deadly poison.

'This stibnite had come from the mullock heap of an ancient, disused stibnite mine that the dust and years had camouflaged until it looked somewhat like a natural hillock. Much the same process had overtaken the four-hundred-yard-wide clearing where trees did not grow because the long-overturned surface of this old mine area was almost iron hard.

'That hillock was the highest permanent natural feature of this area. It was several hundred yards from the pens. But it was only a few seconds' flight for the Rosellas to reach the big ironbark trees from it. The birds swallowed their black roughage on the hillock and then flew to the high trees for the night. During the night the stibnite poison slowly but surely had its deadly effect on them.

'The parrots died and dropped. Some of them fell into the pens. There they had been eaten by some big pigs. Soon they also died. It was a slower death for the bigger, stronger pigs, but equally inevitable.'

He was asked later why had other big pigs in the pens not died?

'The explanation is simple,' he rejoined. 'I reported that the pens were good and the pigs well fed. But I also found that it was only sows that died, and I overheard someone say that the only sows that died were those in litter. Well-fed or not, they hungrily devoured the fallen parrots like scavengers because a sow's appetite is positively enormous when it is in litter. In fact, I know that a sow in litter can get to the stage when it will swallow anything – even a brightly-feathered bird.'

6 The Long Count Back

EVEN when his brain was not tormented and inflamed, Arnold Karl Sodeman boasted that he was the most fiendish girl-strangler in the history of Australian crime. Yet it took only two hard-boiled eggs, cooked in a sterilising pan in a university laboratory twenty years earlier, to prove that he was right.

The strange case of the hard casing really began in August, 1914, the very night Sir Edward Grey commented that 'the lights were going out all over Europe.' However, lights still burned brightly in the almost deserted biochemical laboratory of the University of Melbourne. While most of his fellow students were asleep, Charles Anthony Taylor was humming as he tinkered with glass tubes, beakers, warming baths and hard-boiled eggs, indulging his curiosity in some harmless but interesting experiments on the side. But one day, to the astonishment of police and criminologists, they were to provide a powerful link in the investigation of a chain of crimes that shocked Australia.

Arnold Sodeman, outwardly amiable and disarmingly calm, was a schizophrenic whose brutality was responsible for a man-hunt surpassed in intensity only by the later search for the American soldier, Edward Joseph Leonski. He was a good-natured boy of fourteen when Taylor was burning midnight oil in August, 1914. More than a score of years were to pass before Taylor, by then crime chemist for the Crown, turned back to those lonely nights when only his breathing and the bubbling of boiling water broke the silence of a chill laboratory.

* * *

Young Taylor fumbled under his stained white dustcoat that night in 1914 and glanced at his gold fob watch again.

It was one o'clock. The two hen's eggs had been in boiling water long enough, he decided. He cracked the shells. Both eggs were nicely cooked. Yolks set, and albumen white and firm. But Taylor, the dedicated scientist with the touch of an artist and the majestic coolness of an ice-floe, was not hungry. The hard-boiled eggs had no more appeal for him than has cow's milk for many dairy farmers.

He picked up a thin glass tube about twelve inches long and a little thicker than a cigarette. He forced the firm egg white down the tube and crisply snapped off both ends so that the compressed egg white was flush with each broken end of the tube.

A glass beaker stood in a larger glass water bath, kept at constant body temperature – about 98 degrees F. In the beaker were pepsin and hydrochloric acid, the digestive or gastric juices or agents of the human stomach.

Taylor rested the thin white tube in the beaker like a thermometer in its bath. At one-fifteen he took it out and studied the end that had been submerged. The juices had eaten up the tube, dissolving or digesting the firm albumen for less than one-eighth of an inch down from the lip of the tube. Taylor lowered the tube in the beaker fluid again. It was after one-thirty when he removed it for the second time. The agents had then eaten up the tube and dissolved the albumen for nearly a quarter of an inch.

The tests went on almost until dawn. First one end of the tube, then the other. Then a fresh tube, holding different egg white, so that there would be maximum comparison value.

Sleepy but satisfied, Taylor wrote in his diary: 'Digestion experiments, August, 1914 – repeated tests show that normal stomach agents dissolved albumen at the rate of three-eighths of an inch per hour.'

* * *

Sixteen years later, in 1930, a little girl was murdered. She was the first of four to die in the hands of a strangler who used a peculiar, lapped-hand or crossed-thumbs method that was not suspected by police at the time. For the next five years this strangler defied and defeated the best detectives in Victoria. He may not have been caught had he not betrayed himself by one ill-timed remark.

What is more interesting – and this has been known for thirty years to only very few – is that he could have been hanged for only one murder, while three others would have remained 'unsolved,' in the view of several senior police, but for the enthusiasm and thoroughness of the Government Analyst becoming known as 'The Cat.'

Sodeman was a mild-mannered labourer who adored his wife, Doll, and daughter, Joan. But behind his bland mask he was a violent and in some ways pitiable killer.

During the five years the strangler was at large no suspicion fell on him. None outside his immediate family seemed interested in the oval-faced, calm-featured labourer with the gentle eyes that did not reflect or mirror the storms of his brain. Only he knew of the turbulent, sleepless nights when he was haunted by the knowledge that his father, grandfather and grand-uncle had died insane.

Before he was arrested three innocent men had been charged with his crimes. Their lives were in real jeopardy for a time, and each was finally released in turn in circumstances that revolted all Australia and led to stormy scenes in Government circles, and to bitter and almost savage remonstrations from thousands of the outraged defenders of the innocent.

Sodeman's daughter, Joan, was only two when he committed his first murder, the one that later was to be linked so curiously with the hard-boiled eggs experiment.

On the warm afternoon of Saturday, November 9, 1930, Sodeman ambled up to Mena Griffiths, aged twelve, while she was playing on the swings at Fawkner Park, South Yarra, which is close to the broad, tree-sheltered avenues on Melbourne's famous boulevard, St. Kilda Road. He fobbed off Mena's sister and other playmates by giving them pennies to buy sweets, and then coaxed Mena away on the pretext that she could run an errand for him.

Next day, two youths out bird-nesting found Mena's body on the bathroom floor of a vacant house in Wheatley Road, Ormond, a quiet residential suburb about six miles from Fawkner Park. The body was scantily clad. The girl had been strangled, trussed, and gagged with a piece of her singlet.

Several weeks later the police arrested Robert James McMahon, who was thirty-six, in Sydney, and charged him with the murder. McMahon's impassioned denials were ignored. He faced an identification line-up at Melbourne police headquarters and was alarmed and shocked when two married women of Glenhuntly and Brighton suburbs, and a South Yarra engineer, all swore positively that he was the man they saw on a bus near Fawkner Park the day Mena died.

Desperately McMahon entreated the police to believe that he had been in Leeton, in outback New South Wales, that day. The police and the coroner were not impressed by his denials or his defence, and he was committed for trial on the charge of murder.

But one man was stirred by McMahon's apparent earnestness, Mr C. H. Book, Crown Prosecutor of that decade, and still considered one of the fairest and most perceptive of all time. Book successfully used all his official influence to have McMahon released temporarily in his custody, and then personally escorted him to Leeton, 378 miles west of Sydney. In that sweltering Riverina township Book found twelve reliable men, ranging from a pastrycook to a Scoutmaster and a Salvation Army officer, who proved that McMahon was in that area the day Mena died.

Even this did not clear McMahon completely in the opinion of some police, but it held their official hand until tragedy for another girl changed McMahon's luck. He had been under arrest for more than two months when the killer struck again, with the same brutish characteristics of the Mena Griffiths murder.

During the evening of January 10, 1931, the body of slim, sixteen-year-old Hazel Wilson was found on a vacant allotment near her home in Melton Avenue, Ormond. She had been strangled with a stocking and then gagged, and her hands had been tied behind her back.

Many official faces became scarlet. McMahon was promptly

released, but he received no compensation for the misery of seventy-six days in gaol.

After three months the police were still at a dead end. More than a hundred persons had been questioned closely. The coroner recorded an open verdict, and, incredible as it seems, the rewards offered for the capture of the killer rose no higher than a miserable £50. This miserly attitude to the public's interests did not produce one useful whisper.

And so, for the next four years, Sodeman apparently lived a fairly normal and undisturbed life. He was contented enough and loved at home. His wife had been told much earlier that he had two convictions for misdemeanours, but she did not allow these lapses to ruffle the tranquillity of the home.

Sodeman, for his part, never spoke a word about his past, or contributed news about his daily movements or behaviour. But the hidden facts were that, as Harry Phillips, he had been charged eleven years earlier with attempted robbery under arms at the Melbourne railway station of Surrey Hills. He fled after shooting the assistant-stationmaster in the hand and side, and was later sentenced to three years' imprisonment on French Island. Doll and Joan, and his friends and neighbours and even the police he met, did not even have a suspicion that he had escaped and was sentenced to another year when recaptured.

These facts were not to emerge until 1936, after two more girls had died, and when twenty thousand persons had been interviewed by the police, when mothers throughout territory of a hundred thousand square miles had lived in dread for their daughters' safety, and when the Victoria Police Department had received one of the biggest shakedowns in its history.

The first two unsolved girl murders had almost been forgotten by New Year's Day, 1935, when Ethyl Belshaw vanished. She was a pretty twelve-year-old with long fair hair. She disappeared from among about eight thousand holiday-makers at Inverloch, a seaside and tourist resort at Anderson's Inlet, eighty miles south-east of Melbourne.

When seen last she had been happily licking an icecream as she talked to a slim man on a bicycle. Next day, her body was found in long grass and tea-tree scrub about three hundred yards on the beach side of the Inverloch-Leongatha Road. Her hair was splayed out over the bracken. Her face and legs were cut and battered. She had been trussed hand and foot, strangled manually, and a stocking had been rammed down her throat.

A reward of £500 was offered for the arrest of the murderer, and an Aborigine blacktracker was rushed to the area only to be thwarted by the drenching rain that had fallen overnight.

About eleven thousand people were questioned, including everyone who had been with Ethyl's party, and among these was Arnold Karl Sodeman.

The late Inspecting-Superintendent Jeremiah O'Keeffe, who was a senior-detective on the Sodeman case, once told me that none of the interrogators, including himself, had the slightest suspicion of Sodeman's treble guilt when they checked his movements for that day.

Suspicion fell on another member of Ethyl's party, an eighteen-year-old apprentice, Gordon Herbert Knights. He was charged with the murder, but the charge would not stick, and when the police realised as much, they returned dispiritedly to a fear-swept stretch of coast rich in beauty and barren in clues. They were still hunting for Ethyl's killer nearly a year later when 'The Strangler' struck again.

Six-year-old June Rushmer was found dead at Leongatha, only about sixteen miles north-east of Inverloch.

Sodeman was then working at a Victorian Country Roads Board construction camp sixteen miles outside that township. His workmates there had seen no outward sign of his mental disturbance, especially when enhanced by a few glasses of beer that would scarcely affect a normal man.

Before he retired that painstaking investigator Senior-Detective Fred Delminico told me: 'When we arrested him, Sodeman told me he had for long been haunted by knowing that, after eight glasses of beer, he could not control the impulse to strangle girls.'

Sodeman had had that amount to drink on the afternoon of December 1, 1936. He picked up June Rushmer in the Leongatha township, and she went with him willingly because she was a playmate of Sodeman's little daughter, Joan. He put

June on his bicycle, and he strangled her beneath a tea-tree in McPherson Lane, a half-mile from her holiday home.

Several persons informed the police they had seen a man on a bicycle talking to the girl not long before she died. The faint impressions of a bicycle's wheels were detected in the lane, but the trail vanished.

A few nights later, when the manhunt was at its peak, Sodeman was as quiet as ever. He was seated round a camp-fire as his workmates discussed the tragedy. His cycle was only a few yards away. As he stirred the gum logs, one labourer, without any malice or suspicion of the awful truth, badgeringly said to Sodeman: 'By the way, Arnold, I saw you riding your bicycle down the street that day.'

Those fifteen words were the beginning of the end for Arnold Sodeman. The banter was lost on him. His blandness fell away. His mates started almost unbelievingly as he threw down his mug of billy tea and stalked towards his tent.

'No you bloody well didn't!' he shouted back angrily. 'I wasn't near the bloody joint, I tell you!'

It was most unlike the normal behaviour of affable, placid, likable Arnold Sodeman. Several of his mates looked questioningly at each other. They talked about it for a few minutes, then shrugged and thought no more of it.

But not one man.

He sat alone at the dying fire long after the others were on their stretcher beds. A gong was ringing in his mind, for he was certain he had seen Sodeman in the town that day, and riding his bicycle.

Why was Arnold so upset? he asked himself. Why couldn't he have grinned and accepted the joke for what it was?

The next day he visited the police.

Sodeman was struck dumb when the police came for him. He could understand the bleakness in their eyes. He was crushed and bewildered as the ghastly succession of his crimes flicked through his brain.

He tried to bluff it out, and he tried well. He gave the detectives such a long and detailed account of his movements during the Sunday June had died that they withdrew to check his alibi.

But by the afternoon they were back. 'You realise this looks bad for you?' they said pointedly.

'I know nothing about it,' Sodeman insisted.

He was taken to the police station of a township now electrified by the news of an arrest. Crowds surged in from the bush. One angry mob voted to lynch him and milled threateningly round the shack where he was being questioned.

As the mob fever mounted Sodeman broke down and confessed to the murder of June Rushmer. He was still recapitulating his attack on her in detail when the detectives broke up the interview to get him away from the mob by a back door. He was hurried to Melbourne by a fast car.

'I made a run towards June,' he said. 'She ran into a bush. I ran after her and caught her round the neck, and she began to scream. I held her by the neck and she went limp all of a sudden. I then took off her bloomers and stuffed them into her mouth. I got her belt from her frock and tied it over her mouth and round the back of her head. I then tore a strip off her dress and tied her hands behind her back and left her lying face downwards. I can't say why I did this to June Rushmer. I realised I had done a dreadful act and I went round to the house of Mr Pigdon afterwards to try to show I was away from the scene.'

His confession to the murder was underlined when he wrote this message to his wife:

'Dear Doll, I have confessed my mania and will pay for my sin. Please don't make any effort to obtain counsel for me as I will plead guilty. I want you to put all the money available to your own and Joan's use. May God be always with you and forgive the harm I have done. *P.S.* Love to Joan.'

Then wearily, yet strangely relieved, Sodeman confessed his other hideous crimes.

'There were also the other three,' he blurted to the police. 'Mena Griffiths . . . Hazel Wilson . . . Ethyl Belshaw.'

'You're only boasting,' a senior officer told him. 'We don't believe you could have been that man.'

'I was,' Sodeman urged. 'I killed the four of them like this.'

He showed his listeners how he locked his thumbs together to exert maximum pressure with his palms.

He had been charged only with the murder of June Rushmer. But his persistence finally convinced the detectives on the case that at least an effort should be made to check his story.

They did not know then that Sodeman had been suffering for years from lepto-meningitis, an affliction causing brain tissue to be inflamed by alcohol, and that this had provided his homicidal mania. But they had no doubt that he would hang for the Leongatha murder.

'Tell us what you did,' he was invited.

'I bought Mena Griffiths food before I killed her,' Sodeman said. 'We went towards Chapel Street and got a tram, went down to the shops near the St Kilda Esplanade. I bought her some loquats. . . .'

His listeners stiffened when they heard this. There were probably no more than six men who knew that Mena was found with the remains of loquats in her stomach. That detail had been held back from the press in the hope that the information might prove useful in the future.

'What else?' Sodeman was asked.

'And fish and chips,' he continued. 'I think I can show you the shop I took her to before I went with her to Ormond.'

'We'll try to check your story,' one of the sceptical detectives said. 'If we blow you out we'll know that, for reasons of your own, you're only boasting about these other deaths. But if your statement can be proved, you have put your head in the noose again, because only the man who murdered Mena more than five years ago could know where she was taken that afternoon, exactly what she ate, and when.'

The city morgue was called and a question asked. What was the surest way of checking on Mena Griffiths' last meal? Try the Government Analyst, was the suggestion.

* * *

And so 'The Cat' came to reach up to the dusty files that had lain on his crowded top shelf for years. The five-year-old file he opened on his table was wrapped carefully in ordinary brown paper which was marked boldly: 'Mena Griffiths. Murdered. 1930.'

'My official report back in November, 1930, should decide

this argument,' he told the detectives who called on him. 'These report pages, written by me at the time, show that when Mena Griffiths was murdered the Government pathologist, Dr Crawford Mollison, sent me the contents of her stomach. I checked for poisons. None was present. Not a trace of any. I told Dr Mollison that her stomach had been normal and that the main contents were French-fried potato chips, loquats, cherries and a little amount of fish.

'Mena must have been quite hungry the afternoon she died,' Taylor continued. 'Perhaps it was the promise of potato chips that prompted her to go with Sodeman. That is not for me to say. But, whatever the case, little Mena certainly did bolt those chips down. At the time of my examination I wrote that she had bitten them in half and swallowed most without chewing them at all. As you know, the Australian potato chip is somewhat different from many fried overseas. Ours usually are perhaps three or so inches long, and around half an inch square. The fried, fatty casing of such a potato chip is more resistant to the stomach's gastric or digestive juices than the softer, white, cooked potato inside that fried casing.

'I noticed at the time of my examination that her stomach juices had digested the white potato at the bitten ends of the potato chips. These juices had eaten their way up the potato casing "tubes" for at least a quarter of an inch. I took into account the possible function of the enzymes, which are secreted by the digestive glands, immediately after her death. Now, when I was making this examination and report five years ago, I recalled long experiments about the stomach's digestive properties and agencies I conducted when I was a science student at Melbourne University some sixteen years earlier.

'The point is this. The rates of digestive process for this cooked potato and for firm, hard-boiled white of egg are close enough to be considered as identical. The fried casing had the same relationship to the enclosed cooked potato of the chip as that glass tube had to the egg white during my 1914 experiments. That egg white I tested many times had digested at the rate of three-eighths of an inch per hour. The potato inside Mena's broken chips was about a quarter of an inch eaten out.

Therefore at the time Mena was murdered I submitted my estimate that she had eaten the meal of chips some forty or so minutes before she died. Here is documentary proof of that. Have you retraced with Arnold Sodeman the route he says he took with Mena that day – that is, from the time she first began to eat the chips until he choked her?'

The detectives said they had. Their trip had started at St Kilda, where Sodeman pointed out the fish and chip shop, and continued by bus to Ormond railway station, thence to McKinnon and Wheatley Roads.

'And,' asked 'The Cat,' 'remembering Sodeman's claim that he grabbed Mena by the throat immediately they entered the deserted house, what was the elapsed time of your journey?'

Any detective who had arrived sceptical had by now banished his last lingering suspicion that Sodeman had been bragging or wandering in his mind.

'We took just on forty minutes!' Taylor's visitors told him.

'Thank you,' said 'The Cat.'

During his last few days in the condemned cell Sodeman was apathetic about his fate. On June 1, 1936, he was hanged at Pentridge, the Metropolitan Gaol at Coburg, a Melbourne suburb. A post-mortem revealed that he suffered from lepto-meningitis, a chronic inflammation of the tissue covering the brain.

7 Death in Small Bites

'COUNT me as one of the numerous police officers who acclaim Taylor as the most sagacious Australian crime chemist of our time.'

This tribute came from Assistant-Commissioner Noel Wilby, a veteran of at least a hundred murder investigations, who was catapulted over the heads of senior officers to attain his present rank.

Wilby was one of the many students who, as up-and-coming detectives, sat at the feet of the master when he took his course at Australia's first detective training school. The school was one of the Alexander Mitchell Duncan innovations, and it has been followed by the police officers' college introduced by Duncan's successor, the late Major-General S. H. Porter.

The school came when it was needed most, and though inevitably and irreverently it is more popularly known as 'Bonehead,' it has become a university of crime investigation for chosen students from most Australian States, New Zealand, Fiji, Borneo, Pakistan and Africa.

'Taylor's knowledge is enormous,' Wilby has confirmed. 'But also, by simple down-to-earth demonstrations, he indelibly branded in our minds the importance of trifles and the need to consider every move and word. Police here were lucky to have had that man. I often wonder what the force could have done without him.

'One day he put a glass beaker before our class.

' "Here is a fluid with a revolting taste," he said. "But this is one of the many experiments we must do. Now follow me in every move."

'He clenched his right fist so that only the middle finger was projecting. He dipped it deep in the fluid and then put the finger in his mouth.

' "This may be deadly poison," he announced. "But you must have faith in me. Every man will do that now, and tell me what the taste reminds him of."

'Thirty students groaned, spat and shuddered as they tasted the liquid. But none could give the scientist a definition of the taste, only that it was the most offensive they had experienced. Finally one piped up and asked: "Well, sir, what does it remind you of?"

' "I haven't an idea," Taylor said.

' "But you tasted it too!" the student complained.

' "I did nothing of the sort," Taylor retorted. "Certainly you saw me put a finger in the beaker. But, you see, that was not the finger I put in my mouth."

'Then,' said Assistant-Commissioner Wilby, 'Taylor continued with some real gems of perception that enthralled his class.'

* * *

Usually Taylor's lectures dealt with crime because the fight against it was to be the detectives' major business. But he had enthralling yarns to tell behind the scenes, like those about fish, berries, dough and sugar.

These were not the limited ingredients of an Australian sundowner's meal. They are keywords in Taylor's memoirs that I have chosen at random to show that the scientist's career worked as much in the interests of the peace-loving man as it did against those who broke the law.

The following three tales of decent folk who ate and died did not hit the headlines like the Colin Ross and Leonski murder mysteries. The warnings they whispered were lost among the strident clamourings of a world that was on the march to war. But they show the crime chemist as a truly human person.

Many believe that one of Taylor's greatest contributions to science and the welfare of his fellow-men was the pioneer work he undertook in several fields. Indeed, he did it so often, in fields affecting so many, that even if he did not come to be actually taken for granted his work was often accepted as the expected thing for any scientist to achieve.

It has become a convenient belief that lightning does not strike in the same place twice. However, it is sometimes only the recurrence of disaster that shatters complacency and highlights achievement.

Take, for example, the case of the happy family which, in 1939, went for a holiday to Corner Inlet, an almost landlocked bay on the south-east coast where the enormous gums of the Gippsland forests brood over the Southern Ocean and Tasman Sea. They caught fish with cheap handlines, took them up to the beach-front shack, and fried them for tea. About an hour later the thirty-year-old mother died in agony and some of her family were desperately ill.

No one knew why. So the bush police, following routine, asked for the help of the Government Analyst.

Foul play was not suspected. At least, there were no strong suspicions of it at the time. But, whatever the cause of death, the local doctors refused to certify it until they were given solid proof of it.

Taylor first examined specimens from the dead woman's stomach. Then he called for the skeletons of the fried fish. In accordance with police ritual almost everywhere, they had not been touched until the cause of death had been confirmed. Taylor knew the family had been poisoned, and he was intrigued because he knew that the heat of cooking usually destroyed most of even the most powerful poisons. If, therefore, someone had tried to poison this family, it was most likely that the attempt would have been foiled by heat.

He went over the dinner plates one by one, applying the knowledge of bones and vertebrae he had acquired as a medical student before medico-legal chemistry became his life. First he noticed that the bone structure of one skeleton – it was on the dead woman's plate – was slightly different from that of the other fish of the same size. It belonged to a fish head in which later he found a peculiar tooth formation.

All the family had eaten samples of this fish. But the mother, after giving all a taste, had retained the remainder. This, Taylor decided, was the key to the problem.

Next day, with help from museum specialists, he identified this fish. It was *Tetraodontidae*, meaning four-toothed, a rare, deadly, slow-swimming fish with four teeth fused in the upper and lower jaws. The poison in this fish is so deadly that it has not yet been identified and, unlike cyanide and other poisons which evaporate when heated, persists in a highly toxic form even after frying.

Japanese and Russians have tried many times to identify the poison by trial – and almost error. Two Japanese, one a professor, having taken all precautions, came close to death after deliberately swallowing only tiny portions of the fish.

Here is the sequel:

On March 22, 1959 – some twenty years after the Corner Inlet incident – Mrs Maria Bachi, forty, of Toorak, Melbourne, and her husband were rushed by ambulance from the Dromana foreshore to the Alfred Hospital in Melbourne. Both were given blood transfusions and both hovered on the danger list for several days.

It had been established that they had eaten a little fish, and then it was said to have been a toad, or toady, fish. Doctors agreed that its poison was very virulent.

'But,' said one official during the struggle to save the patients' lives, 'no one here has ever died from eating this fish.'

I showed the published account of the case to Taylor soon after the couple had rallied and were beginning a slow struggle to recovery.

He smiled and shook his greying head.

'The statement is flatly wrong,' he said. 'It was *Tetraodontidae* all over again. Those who make such statements should be more responsibly informed.'

There is a lesson in the next case for all newly-weds, for all planning attractive gardens, and for those who have left theirs untended.

Taylor was told that a boy of about five had died in strange circumstances at Bacchus Marsh, a rich English-type grazing district thirty miles north-west of Melbourne. It seemed he had played all day in the town streets with his pals, had eaten a heavy meal in the evening, and soon afterwards had collapsed and died suddenly.

But even a post-mortem, when every other measure had failed, did not disclose the cause of death. Specimens of the boy's stomach were then sent down to the Government Analyst.

The versatile 'Cat' had once been a student of flora as well as fauna. He strolled into my back garden not long ago, glanced up at a sixty-foot nuisance tree and said: 'Better get that out. Grevillia, Queensland silky oak. A fine tree in sub-tropical forests, but they grow very brittle in the south. Too brittle to be used for furniture down here, and the limbs may break in storms.'

Which was exactly the definition I was given later by timber experts when planning to have the tree removed because its limbs were fracturing in winds. 'A valuable tree up north,' they said. 'But it's commercially useless here.'

This was the type of knowledge Taylor was applying as he detected, among the remains of the boy's last meal, what appeared to be specks of a black vegetable. But it was not related to any items on the list sent down by police of anything the boy was known to have eaten during the twenty-four hours before he died. Nor did it resemble anything the other members of the family had eaten in that time.

In his Spring Street office at midnight, Taylor telephoned the police sergeant at Bacchus Marsh with a strange request. Would the sergeant take his notebook to the vicinity of the boy's home, have a good look at the surrounding district, and write down the names of every vegetable, tree, shrub, plant or hedge in the gardens of houses and parks nearby?

It was a mammoth order for a sergeant more accustomed to making entries in his station duty, occurrence and correspondence books, and catching thieves. But he was not the type to argue that his knowledge of botany would not meet requests. Before noon next day he telephoned a commendable list to Melbourne. Taylor became interested in one item only.

'You say there's an ordinary privet hedge at the boy's front fence?' he asked the sergeant. 'And you say it's tall, straggling, and apparently running wild? Now I see. I really do!'

Taylor nodded his wise old head. It was the case of a small boy, lacking the caution of his elders, who had innocently plucked and eaten the deadly berries of an ordinary common or garden privet hedge that had flowered after being allowed to grow too long.

Shortly before his death Taylor lived in a red-brick house only six miles from the city. It was planted heavily with roses, shrubs and bulbs. But there had never been a privet there.

My own sole specimen has since been a regular customer for the shears!

* * *

About eight months later two parents watched their lad playing happily with other children at Ouyen, an agricultural township of the vast, wheat-growing Mallee plains. Suddenly he collapsed, groaning. Horrified, they saw him jerk convulsively and die. Doctors and police were baffled, and the parents mystified through several grief-stricken days.

'The Cat' told me he also was puzzled for many hours when he analysed and tested the contents of the boy's stomach and found definite symptoms of antimony poisoning. He knew, from experience as a mining assayer and teacher many years earlier, that there was no likelihood of natural deposits of antimony in the Ouyen district. That fact, and the conviction that the boy could not have been poisoned deliberately in the known time sequences, were the most important features of the case, because they narrowed Taylor's theory to the probability that the boy had accidentally swallowed the deadly poison.

But where, how and why? These were the three questions requiring answers. There were no poisons of that nature at his house or in or near his school.

Taylor slowly developed a theory as he worked late one night, mentally eliminating all possible sources of the poison and awaiting the report of a detective who was trying to reconstruct the boy's last movements before he died. The detective found that the lad had played marbles on the footpaths, and Red Indians in the streets. He had swung on boughs, run, skipped and jumped, gone to a playmate's paddock for a ball game, returned home for an ordinary lunch of cold meat and pickles, bowled a hoop for a while, sat in a gutter, scrambled over a rubbish tip, and gone home for a wash.

'All the things any kid might do,' the detective said.

The analyst agreed. Particularly about scrambling over a rubbish tip. 'Send me several samples from different parts of it,' he requested.

Specimens arrived in his laboratory next day. Taylor pored over them for two hours. He ran them through a dozen chemical and microscope tests and then set one specimen aside for a special test. It was a sticky, syrupy substance, was sweet, and reacted promptly to antimony tests.

But how did such muck get to a country rubbish tip? Taylor's fresh tests showed that some grey smears were made by baking powder and water. But what possible relationship could antimony, a killer, have with these?

There was only one way to find out. It was hardly feasible that any housewife would trouble to discard baking powder on a country tip. But he asked a country detective by long-distance telephone if there was a baker near the town, and learned there was. Taylor then requested the detective to call on the baker with some questions.

When they were answered, 'The Cat' was again able to report the solution of a mystery. He wrote:

'A baker in Ouyen had been troubled by ants in his bakehouse. He set out an anti-ant preparation which was very effective, then swept out his bakehouse and the sweepings, including the dead ants and the preparation that had attracted them, were just dumped on the district tip.

'A little boy passed by. He fell over, perhaps, or maybe he was happy just to sprawl among the rubbish for a time. Whatever the case, his fingers were stickied accidentally by the discarded preparation, and he began to saunter home to wash. On the way he sucked his finger. He enjoyed the deceptively sweet taste – unfortunately, that of antimony in the anti-ant preparation. As any other little boy would have done, he sucked his fingers again. And then he died.'

8 *Baby-face, the Mad Yank*

It was just plain but painful bad luck that Private Edward Joseph Leonski, the grinning 'Mad Yank' who terrorised a million people during the wartime blackout, slipped through the one hole in a strong police net and was not arrested before he had murdered his last attractive victim. He actually came face to face with the only policeman who could have recognised him, and the memory or perception of that policeman failed him at the very moment the hunt had reached its crisis. Leonski cheekily strolled past him to seek more prey.

Because that happened another pretty woman went to a ghastly death in oozing mud and freezing rain.

She should not have died. But her fate had already been decided by the tremendous difference between 'It's *not* him' and 'Well, it *could* be him.'

Another object lesson of this story is that it was through priceless luck and the coincidence of timing, after really gruelling weeks of investigation, that Leonski was surprised and captured at the very moment when the weary detectives were hoping they might temporarily suspend the search for him that day.

Leonski was surrounded quite suddenly. But when he found himself inside a bristling circle of US sub-machine-guns, instead of walking out on leave to kill in the night again, he quickly recovered from the shock, and gave the police the same saucy grin that had intrigued them when they saw him shaking pepper into his liquor at a nearby hotel only a few days earlier.

This is largely the secret history of the Leonski case. The facts of his first escape and arrest have never been disclosed, not even at the American court-martial which ordered him to be put to death, because they have been shared by very few. This number did not even include Charles Anthony Taylor, who later was to have on his microscope platform the tiny grains of gravel and mud that would send Leonski to an Australian gallows trap.

The facts will interest those who have tried to analyse the strange personality of Leonski. They prove he must have been one of the most insouciant split-personality murderers in the long history of unlawful killing.

Leonski prowled the blacked-out streets when the Japanese invasion scare was at its peak, when Australia was whispering about a last-ditch 'Brisbane Line,' when bombs were raining on Darwin, when the Australian toll of murder, violence and vice had soared alarmingly, and when nerves were ragged and the crime-fighting strength of the police had been reduced by Service enlistments and the added duties of ARP control.

He caused an anxious Australian manhunt that can be compared in magnitude only to the search for the kidnapper of little Graeme Thorne in Sydney, in 1960. His name was an embarrassment to every American Serviceman in Australia.

People's eyes goggled when they saw this American soldier drinking in the city bars, and he went to many. But the one he seemed to favour most was at the east end of the city. It is one where, the barmen and barmaid still insist, two men of widely opposite ranks, stations and ambitions had drunk a little in the same corner at different times and then gone to find fame their different ways.

One, the barmen say, was Prince Philip, then Prince Philip of Greece, Lieutenant, RN.

The other man seen in the corner where the Prince had had a glass with visiting naval friends was the powerful and springy soldier they had reason to remember as 'Baby-face, the Mad Yank.'

He seemed to be 'just a good guy,' then. A strange one, though. He mixed beer, whisky, brandy, ice-cream, ketchup, mustard, vinegar, hot peppers and anything else to hand, and drained his glass with apparent relish. Women giggled when they saw him standing on his hands and walking for several minutes, sometimes for as long as a quarter of an hour. They did not hear his whispered talk of werewolves howling, of split personalities, of poltergeists and Jekyll and Hyde. Only a few noticed the glazed look in his eyes at times, the clenchings of his abnormally powerful hands, his random talk of 'soft, soft women,' 'nice voices,' and how he cried the day he left Texas for duty overseas.

'Ah, just a strange American,' they said. 'A good-time Yank down under.'

That was only a few chilling weeks before a US Army court-martial described him as 'Baby-face, but vicious underneath.'

* * *

Melbourne – staid, dignified and outwardly conservative, yet trembling with young passion and unbridled emotion when people like the Beatles come – was described by the American evangelist Dr Billy Graham as one of the most moral cities in the world. Dr Graham did not get around and peep behind the masquerade.

For the past few years Melbourne has had one of the highest pro-rata homosexual ratings of any of the many cities I know. Sex crimes and aberrations are among the 'Big Three' in regular crime reviews. Scores of girls have been driven from the streets, but the city and suburbs are studded around a 'Golden Circle' of sleazy night-clubs and rotten honky-tonks where the lowest forms of prostitution thrive.

The mass-immigration programme has brought new problems, and it is no secret officially that gangs of southern Europeans – some ruthless members of a Mafia-type society – have trafficked fourteen-year-old girls to country districts under conditions no less evil than a Continental or Eastern white-slave trade. Or that half-caste aboriginal girls – only fifteen years old – have been brought over State lines and marketed in Melbourne.

Despite pretences, Melbourne always managed an ugly record for vice, violence, conspiracy, intrigue and murder. It could, therefore, have appealed to Leonski's twisted ego that he still holds the title as the local arch-fiend of the century. None of Victoria's many murderers has killed, and tried to kill or maim, with such lightning thrusts and lunges. None was a greater threat. None attempted nor committed more murders in the time. Certainly none, including Arnold Karl Sodeman, had more capacity for terror and blood and was more indifferent to the consequences.

Whenever I think of Leonski I recall a statement made to me in Washington by the then Attorney-General of the United States, Mr William Rogers. 'By far our greatest problem these days is the juvenile delinquent,' he said. 'We are concerned not only with the number of them. Of greater concern is the fact that they are becoming menaces greater than the gangsters of the Al Capone era. At least the Capones had motives – hijacking, lust for power and profit, bootlegging and gangland domination. But many of our youths and girls today are committing atrocious crimes with no motive we can see.'

Leonski, only twenty-four when hanged, may have fitted into that category. He was a 'war baby,' born in the last year of the First World War. He was one of the vanguard of the world's aimless, brutally sadistic young people who were left to beat out their own ways in a post-war world too neurotic, nervy, selfish, security-hungry and often leaderless to understand the symptoms or correct the drift.

Leonski also may inherently have been a killer who would have committed these or similar crimes whatever the times or economic conditions. Both his parents were insane and had been in the same asylum at the same time. Like Sodeman, too, he may have suffered from a terrible but rarely apparent derangement, lepto-meningitis. With Leonski it must be remembered that, much as with Sodeman, psychiatrists had declared him usually sane, but a roused killer under the urge of drink.

Still, what actually motivated him is not clear and determined and probably never will be. Leonski took that secret with him to his grave. A few official papers, and others in my possession, are the only records in Australia of his crimes, and the only remaining pointers to his character. As with his cremated ashes, most other documents were sent to his homeland long ago.

But one thing is clear. It was not suppression or repression that spurred him to murder women and try to mutilate other girls. Melbourne was almost a wide-open city when he came to it. Its morals were never lower in our times and many of its population, permanent and floating, never reached a looser, more debased, lustful and dissolute level. Every opportunity for a debauched mind was there, as I can testify.

The menace of Leonski was greater because he chose to be a blackout prowler who not once left the police an apparent motive for his crimes. Motive always is the big question mark in murder. Find that and you often find the man.

It was difficult for the police to accept at the time that the prowler was killing for the few shillings he obtained. It was equally difficult later for them to accept completely Leonski's claims that he became a fiend because he 'wanted those sweet voices of his victims.' No psychologist or psychiatrist has found the answer since.

Leonski was, and remains, the enigma whose calm indifference left everyone associated with him aghast and amazed.

Taylor was not one of those who helped to put the handcuffs on Leonski. This was done by Sid McGuffie, Fred Adam, Harry Carey, Harry McMennemin, Ernest Craig, Frank Lyon, William Mooney and those who worked with them. They narrowed down a wide field by elimination after an immense check on almost every American Serviceman in the State's eighty-eight thousand square miles.

Taylor was working in his office, testing bloodstains and some unpromising clues, when Leonski's three known victims were throttled and those who had miraculously survived his other attacks were choking out reports of the good-looking prowler who had grinned and then gripped them by the throat with appalling ferocity. Taylor was still working in his office when the police pointed an accusing finger at Private Leonski and said: 'That's the man we want.'

In fact, Taylor had played only a small and very formal part in the big trackdown.

But none of the police who brought Leonski to his army trial deny that, although they figuratively dropped the noose over Leonski's shoulders, it was Taylor who finally pulled it tight.

The sands of Leonski's life ran out when Taylor built a mountain of proof from a few grains of mud and gravel.

Leonski died without disclosing when he made the first attack which gave the south of Australia its most jittery crime wave in more than a hundred years. He was charged with three murders, each on a dark, stormy night. But some say that his tally of victims murdered could have been five and that among his other victims may have been at least one whose killing is still unsolved. Whatever the total, we know that several other women were fantastically lucky to escape death by seconds, and that 'Baby-face' began his demoniacal prowl about two months before the first of his known victims died. There is little doubt now, for example, that a Mrs Doreen Justice was one of the first to feel the strangler's vice-like fingers around her throat. Nor is there doubt that Leonski's toll would have been much greater at this time had he not been under a month's detention for a misdemeanour.

Mrs Justice lived at Glebe, Sydney, but came to Melbourne for a health holiday in January, 1942. She was one of several women who narrowly escaped being throttled by him, but two months were to pass before she reported her experience to police. In fact, it was not until after Leonski had begun to kill that Mrs Justice, back in Sydney, realised how lucky she had been.

At this stage the known movements of Leonski will be easier to follow from the official statements of witnesses or near-victims, whether they were taken before or after his arrest. This is the account of Mrs Justice after she returned from Melbourne to New South Wales and was interviewed there by the chief of the Sydney CIB, Detective-Superintendent Matthews, at the request of the Victorian CIB.

Leonski had not then been arrested. In fact, the prowler's identity was a mystery. But Mrs Justice had read two accounts of Melbourne murders in Sydney newspapers since her return, and she knew in her heart that the killer still being sought must have been the man she faced one night about two months before. Only the repulsive parts, in which she outlined her attacker's onslaught, have been deleted from her report, which runs:

'I am a married woman, twenty-two years of age, and residing with my husband, Mr Percy Neville Stewart Justice, at 5, Leichardt Place, Glebe. I have one child nineteen months old.

'About the end of January, 1942, I went to Melbourne at the instigation of my doctor, as he informed me that it would improve my health. The baby accompanied me. My husband and I had previously resided in Melbourne, but we came to Sydney about six months ago. On arrival in Melbourne, I stayed at the Federal Hotel for about a fortnight and then I took a flat at 80, Gray Street, St Kilda.

'I took the flat under the name of Mrs Justice about Thursday, the 5th February, 1942. About the middle of March I had been into the city to do some shopping and I left the baby with my mother, Mrs Pollard, 27 Ferris Place, Albert Park. I arrived home to my flat between 5.30 and 6 p.m. I put my key in the lock of the door and opened it, when a man walked up behind me and pushed me into my flat on to a couch that was directly in front of the entrance.

'He slammed the door after coming into the flat. I turned round off the couch and stood on to my feet. The man said: "Take it easy, baby. Don't scream and everything will be all right. If you do scream, I will choke you. I like your line. I have taken a fancy to you – and what I want I get."

'I said: "What are you doing here? Get out of here." The man said: "If you don't like my looks, maybe this will tempt you," and he pulled some money out of his trousers pocket.

'He was smiling at me when he said this. I said: "I am not that type of woman and you can get out of here." He said: "That's what you think." His face changed from a smile to a threatening expression, and he grabbed my throat with two hands. He squeezed my throat with his hands and forced me to my knees, and for the moment everything went black. He then took his hands away from my throat and I fell to the floor, and when the man had hold of me by the throat I felt a choking sensation and my tongue protruded from my mouth.

'The man picked me up from the floor from where I had

fallen and carried me towards the bed and went to throw me on the bed. As he did this, I caught hold of the top of the bed and he tried to pull me away from it, placing both hands around my waist and pulling at me.

'I said: "Water." He said: "You are trying to trick me. You are trying to get away." I said: "No. Let me get a drink of water. I am not trying to get away." He then gripped my arm and went with me to the kitchenette. I got a cup and got myself a drink of water. The man stood at the back of me so that I could not get away.

'I got to a door and partly opened it far enough to put my foot in the opening, but the man prevented me from opening it any wider. The man tried to pull me from the door. I heard somebody coming along the passageway towards the entrance of the flat. I called out: "For God's sake, help me!" A woman who came into the passageway, a Mrs O'Neill, a relative of the people who own the flats, came up and said: "What is the matter?" She then saw the man and called out for her husband.

'I then went into Mrs O'Neill's flat, which was next door to mine. Mrs O'Neill called another man. I believe he is her brother-in-law, and he went to my flat and I was informed that he tried to open the door, but it was locked, and the man eventually left my flat by the back door. I then returned to the flat with the brother-in-law of Mrs O'Neill and I found the man's cotton singlet on the floor in the bedroom with a laundry mark E.J.L. (or F.J.L.) thereon.'

This statement, it should be remembered, puts Leonski's known movements in chronological order, and was made after he had been arrested. In effect, six weeks before the first victim died Mrs Justice held the one tangible clue to the prowler's identity. But her understandable shyness and wish to avoid publicity restrained her from handing the police the one clue that could have cut short Leonski's rampage. Her statement continues:

'I was on my own when I found the singlet and I did not show any of the other people in the flat the singlet. I told them that the man had followed me into my flat and tried to get funny with me.

'The following day my throat was very sore and there were

marks where the man's fingers had pressed my throat. I did not inform my mother of the occurrence because I did not want to upset her. I did not explain the matter at all to the landlady because she is a very old woman, but Mrs O'Neill, who is a relative by marriage of the landlady, knew of the occurrence and she and her brother-in-law advised me not to tell the landlady.

'I still continued to live at the flat and I returned to Sydney about a month after the assault and I informed my husband about the matter.

'I had never seen the man prior to the assault. I would describe the man as: About twenty-eight years of age, about five foot ten inches high, well built, about twelve stone weight, pale complexion, sandy-coloured hair, believed to be straight, which was disarranged, pale blue eyes, clean-shaven, medium-featured, firm, well-shaped mouth, exceptionally good teeth, but they may have been false. Definite American accent, dressed in light khaki trousers and shirt, wearing a khaki cap similar in shape to that worn by the United States sailors.

'I could identify the man if I saw him again. The singlet that the man took off in my room has been in my possession since the happening and I brought it back to Sydney with me when I returned. My husband mentioned to me about the women that had been strangled in Melbourne and he reported the matter to the police as my husband read in the paper that a man with the same initials as appeared on the singlet had been charged in Melbourne.'

Madness again stormed into Leonski's skull only a few nights after this attack in March. It was possibly the madness, as was suggested later, of a young man bent on the murder of women older than himself because he had been in love with his brother's wife in America, and she, a few years senior, did not return his love. Whether the diagnosis be true or not, Leonski left no doubt of his intentions the night he accosted a woman at the Glaciarium, on the Yarra bank, near Princes Bridge, and asked her to skate with him.

The woman refused. Unknown by her, he shadowed her from the rink and followed her as she left the tram in the street where she lived at South Melbourne. Putting his hands around her throat, he hissed: 'I was going to kill a girl tonight. You might as well be the one.'

She managed one scream before Leonski's grip tightened. A man in the blackout heard that scream. Leonski heard his running steps, hurled his unconscious victim to the road, and loped away unseen.

No one can explain all of Leonski's movements and behaviour over the following two months, particularly the month following this attack. But May soon became the month that Melbourne will not forget.

This is the known calendar of his crimes during his off-duty nights within the short span of three weeks:

May 2 .. Murder of Ivy McLeod.
9 .. Murder of Pauline Thompson, a policeman's wife.
12 .. Kathleen Elliott almost throttled.
12 .. Only minutes later, Leonski brazenly asked a nearby constable for a cigarette.
12 .. And then stalked on and tried to strangle a Miss Hardy.
14 .. Leonski disturbed by an uncle as he was about to choke the niece.
18 .. Murder of Gladys Hosking.

Again, what happened on those nights is best described by witnesses who survived, and by official accounts after Leonski began to realise, despite his repeated denials, that he was trapped.

On the morning of May 3, 1942, the body of Mrs Ivy McLeod had been found in the recess of a doorway to a shop near the Bleak House Hotel. This corner hotel faces wind-swept Port Phillip Bay at Albert Park, only three miles along the south-east foreshore from Melbourne. Leonski's own statement, which I have before me, dismissed the murder in these few paragraphs:

'I was drinking at the Bleak House Hotel with a number of soldiers. One of these soldiers was McPhillips, from my outfit. I borrowed twenty-four shillings from him. We drank for a while. I don't know how many drinks we had. We were drinking beer and Scotch. Mac left. I don't know what time he left. I had been drinking all day. I know I was high when I went into the hotel.

'I left with an American soldier and a girl. We walked across the street to the beach front and drank a bottle of beer. The other soldier got up and left. I don't know why he left.

'I was alone with the girl. We necked a little bit. I think her name was Pat. We got up and walked back to the corner across the street. The other soldier was waiting there for us. The three of us stood around and talked while waiting for a tram. When the tram came the soldier and the girl got on it and left.

'My tram was a long time in coming. I got to thinking about home and how lonely I was. Then I thought about six Australian civilians who had jumped me one time and choked me until I was almost unconscious. I got tired of waiting and started to walk up Victoria Street. There was a girl standing by a doorway. She smiled. I made some comment about her bag. I took it in my hands and then gave it back to her.

'The girl moved back into the recess and I must have followed her. I had my arms around her neck. I grabbed her by the neck the left side. I changed the position of my hands and grabbed her at the front of the throat.

'I squeezed and she fell rapidly. Her head hit the ground while I still had my hands on her throat. I started to rip and tear her clothes until I came to her belt. I just couldn't rip that belt. I ripped her clothes below the belt and came back to it. The belt made me mad. While I was trying to rip the belt I heard footsteps. I picked up my hat, which had fallen off, put it on. I turned to my right and walked up Victoria Street.

'I didn't look back. I don't remember what time or how I got back to camp.'

At that time he need not have cared. No one could have identified him in the blackout. Melbourne was bursting with American, Filippino and Dutch and other troops, all of whom wore uniforms similar to his own. In any case, it was to be a big year for unsolved murder, one the short-staffed Homicide Squad was hoping would never recur. The body of a near-naked woman in the St Vincent's Hospital grounds, the bodies of two Australian soldiers near the coastal forts – these were only three more of the unsolved crimes.

Had Leonski stopped there, it is more than likely that his secret would have been sealed by silence once he had embarked for service north. But Leonski did not stop. The demons in his brain were spouting flame. He continued to drink heavily. Sometimes he was morose and wept. He had spasms of jubilation, and he had times when he brooded over the newspaper cuttings of his murders which, it was found later, he nursed jealously under his palliasse.

At night he pestered girls at fun parlours and Luna Park on St Kilda Beach. He intercepted them at tram stops and startled them with wild theories on psychology. None of these suspected at the time when they were either recoiling or giggling that this was the fiend who attacked with viciousness that had snapped a woman's spine, broken her skull and cut her brain.

Mrs Pauline Buchan (Coral) Thompson, the pretty brunette wife of a country policeman, First Constable Leslie Thompson, was to be the second of these unfortunates.

About 5.30 p.m. on May 8 Mrs Thompson saw her husband off on a train to Bendigo and returned to the city to keep a secret appointment with an American soldier. He did not appear. Mrs Thompson waited for a while and then met a wandering GI who said his name was Eddie.

Parts of the next four hours they were together are obscure. But Arthur Bliss, a barman, saw her and an American soldier in the lounge of the Astoria Hotel, at the south end of Collins Place, about ten o'clock that night. Bliss, in a statement to me, recalled that until midnight he served them with about a dozen gin squashes. Later, at an identification parade, he was unable positively to recognise Leonski as the man. But he did recall that the soldier he had seen that night 'appeared to have a pleasant face.'

Mrs Thompson's body was found before dawn on the steps of a Spring Street apartment house, near Parliament House, where she had stayed for five days.

Mrs Thompson, who was thirty-nine, had come down from Bendigo eight months earlier to work for the International

Harvester Company during the day, and for 3 AW radio station at night.

Three days after she had been murdered a model of her figure, decked with her clothes and superimposed with a photograph of her face, was prepared at CIB headquarters. Reconstruction photographs were then circulated by the thousand throughout Australia in an all-out effort to find anyone who had seen the woman during her last few hours.

The post-mortem examination by the Government pathologist, Dr Crawford Mollison, revealed death from cardiac inhibition from pressure on the throat, the circular advised. 'She and a well-built American soldier left the Astoria Hotel about midnight. This is the last information gathered to date about her movements.'

Again, gaps are best filled by Leonski's later version:

'I remember now about the girl who was killed in Spring Street. I met her in a restaurant. She was waiting for an order. I asked her if I could sit with her. She smiled and said: "All right." I told her that I would rather have something stronger to drink. She told me that she knew of a place. We walked around a bit. It was raining and we stood in doors. We met a soldier who showed us a place to go and get a drink.

'We were sitting at the table drinking. I bought a few drinks. There was a girl sitting at a table in the corner looking at me. I was looking at her. My girl wanted to shout. I told her when I went broke I would let her shout a drink. She did shout.

'She was singing in my ear. She looked into my eyes and it sounded as if she was just singing for me. She was drinking gin squash. I tasted it, but it was too mild. She said that she was not married. We were talking about life. We got on swell together.

'She asked me if I needed any money. I told her I didn't need any money. We sat around a while and drank. She told me she sang. After I was broke she kept on buying all the drinks. When we left the hotel she picked up her bag.

'She had a nice voice and she sang as we walked along. We turned a corner. There was nobody around. I didn't see anybody. I just heard her voice.

'Then we came to the stone steps. They were long steps. I

grabbed her – I grabbed her. I don't know why. I grabbed her around the neck. She stopped singing.

'I said: "Keep singing. Keep singing." She fell down.

'I got mad and tore at her – tore at her. I tore her apart. There was someone coming across the street. I hid behind a stone wall. I was terrified. My heart was pounding a mile a minute.

'I couldn't bear to look at her. I saw her purse. I knew I had to get back and I didn't have any money. I picked up her purse and put it under my coat. I knew I couldn't go far with such a big purse. I turned left and I ran into an alley. I looked into her purse. There was a lot of things in it.

'I couldn't find the money at first. Everything I touched I smudged. I didn't want to leave fingerprints. I finally found the money. There was two and a half pounds. I dropped the purse. I saw the money under the light. I went to the corner and took a taxi back to the camp. I went to bed, but I did not sleep much. I woke up the next morning with a terrible headache. I looked for a drink straight away. I don't know where I found it. Probably one of the boys had a bottle. They always do.

'She would not sing. How could she sing? Me choking her when I wanted her to sing?'

* * *

That was the last of Leonski's known and proven crimes in the heart of the city and south of it. Throughout the next nine days and nights, a period that shook Melbourne and shattered the crime-hunting records of the nation, Leonski marauded mainly along the tree-lined avenues within a half-mile of his camp, Camp Pell, towards the northern fringe of Melbourne.

Miss Kathleen Elliott, a saleswoman, of 185 Park Street, Parkville, had an ugly encounter with him in the drizzly twilight of May 12, less than four days after Mrs Pauline Thompson died. It was only a few hundred yards from the spot where 'The Mad Yank' soon was to commit the last of his monstrous crimes.

'At 6.20 p.m. I was walking along Wimble Street, from Royal Park, to my home in Park Street,' Miss Elliott related shortly afterwards. 'I was accosted by an American soldier who was wearing a fatigue uniform. He said: "Have you a cigarette?" I said: "No." He said: "Can I walk along with you?' I said: "I suppose I can't stop you."

'He walked with me for about three hundred yards. He said: "We are rationed with cigarettes, we only get one packet a day."

'When I reached the front gate of my home, I opened it and entered, and when I reached the front door, which is about six feet from the gate, I placed the key in the front door, and as I did the soldier said: "Are you going to invite me in?"

'I put him off by saying something about my husband being in. He then suddenly grabbed me by the throat and I screamed. He let me go and ran north along Park Street.

'He was an American soldier, twenty-four years of age, five foot nine or ten inches high, fair hair and complexion, stocky build, dressed in fatigue uniform and cloth cap. Broad nose, broad face, had little or no accent. Gave giggle or chuckle after each sentence.'

Only a few minutes after that encounter, and still only three hundred yards away, Leonski had the nerve to ask a constable for cigarettes and then coolly march off up the road.

Ten minutes later he struck again. He came up behind a Miss Hardy as she was opening the gate of her home and pounced without warning. He seized her neck from behind and exerted all his strength. She managed one scream before she fell, limp and helpless. Again Leonski ran.

Two nights later, May 14, he was out again.

He followed a young woman along Gatehouse Street, in the same Parkville district. He waited until she opened her front door, pushed in behind her, and stalked her menacingly to the kitchen. But suddenly there was a babble of voices. Her uncle appeared in a lobby, and Leonski vanished as quickly as a cat.

Leonski's lust and danger potential now were at their peak. This was the period when he could have been identified and caught, and then Gladys Hosking, a lovely girl standing under an umbrella in the rain, would not have died.

Gladys was a small, cool-skinned girl who worked at the nearby University as secretary to Professor Ernst Johannes Hartung's school of chemistry. She was cultured and popular, but could have had a remote yet uncanny premonition of her fate. I know that, in the last letter she sent to her parents in Western Australia, she wrote of the big American camp at Royal Park and 'how frightened she was to go out in the blackout.'

Mrs Hosking, in her last letter posted in the west on May 11, said she hoped her daughter was 'more contented.'

At 7 a.m. on Tuesday, May 19, 1942, Gladys's near-nude body was found face downwards in a vast sea of mud surrounding air-raid slit trenches near Camp Pell. Leonski had mocked the police and sent her to a pitiless death because she was 'so soft' and he 'wanted that voice.'

His statement read later:

'On Monday night, May 18, I was drinking beer in the Parkville Hotel. When the pub closed I went to the home of a friend with him, and lay on the bed for about thirty minutes. Then I got up and walked out. I walked up the street.

'On the corner I met a girl. It was a small girl. She was carrying an umbrella. It was raining, and I asked her to let me walk along with her. She said: "All right." We walked along the street. We came to her house. I asked her to walk on with me and show me the way to camp. She said: "All right." Soon we came to a very dark part of the street. She stopped and said: "There's the camp over there."

'She had a lovely voice. I wanted that voice. She was leaving to go to the house and I did not want her to go. I grabbed her by the throat. I choked her, I choked her. She didn't even make a sound.

'She was so soft.

'I thought: "What have I done? I will have to get away from here." I then got her to a fence. I got over and pushed her and pulled her by the armpits underneath it. I carried her a short distance and fell in the mud.

'She made funny noises, a kind of gurgling sound. I thought: "I must stop that!" So I tried to pull her dress over her face. I became frightened and started to run away. Then I met a soldier. He asked me where I was going. I told him Royal Park. He said: "Where do you live?" I said: "Area One, near the Zoo." He said: "Go this way."

'I walked a long time and after a while I came to my latrine and walked in, and some soldier asked me: "Where have you been?" I told him I had fallen in the mud. I then went to my tent. I took my muddy clothes off, and got into bed. Next morning I woke and saw the muddy clothes. I thought to myself: "My God, where have I been? What have I done?" I then got up and washed the muddy clothes.'

* * *

Straight from the original files, those are the confessions of the 'good-time Yank down under.'

The cart has been deliberately put before the horse, and his statements tabled before describing the hue-and-cry for him. This was to create a mental image of the strangler. Now, it is important to define the atmosphere of the time, and the events which led tortuously to these confessions. It is equally important, too, to remember that – as so often happens in civil courts these days – these confessions required other evidence to clinch the certainty of his guilt, because, despite these statements, Leonski went to his court-martial pleading not guilty to every charge.

Until the moment Gladys Hosking died Leonski had left very few clues to his identity for the first police on the case: Detective-Sergeant Sid McGuffie and Detective Ernest Craig. The initialled singlet found by Doreen Justice in her St Kilda flat several weeks earlier would have been invaluable, but it was not produced until the killer was behind bars.

Leonski had painstakingly smeared whatever he touched to distort his fingerprints, which could have been checked with the prints in every American Serviceman's paybook. In other cases – even much less threatening ones – Senior-Detective Harry McMennemin and renowned fingerprint expert Alec Martin had patiently flicked through seventeen thousand American paybooks and tested bullets from ten thousand US guns in search for a wanted man. The team was ready to work this way again when the time came.

Although the nine-thousand-mile Australian coastline was then studded with foreign Servicemen wearing uniforms similar to a GI's dress, the police were positive that their quarry was an American. Already they had dubbed him 'The Mad Yank.' The sparse evidence they had, and a fine analysis of many reports about the movements of Americans, made it probable that he had an engaging grin, was very powerful, may have had a yellow or orange flash around his Service cap, and had an extraordinary habit of 'doctoring' his already potent drinks.

The descriptions they had, however, were not enough.

It is a pity that none of the four or five persons furnishing descriptions of the man who probably was 'the blackout strangler' had overlooked one point – he had protruding, jug-handle ears. If only that peculiarity had been noticed in the Astoria Hotel on the night of May 8, when he murdered Pauline Thompson, the manhunt might have ended much sooner. Those ears could have been the essential factor in the massive identification line-ups that spread from the city to camps at Balcombe, the Melbourne Cricket Ground, Camp Pell, Seymour, Ballarat, and further north.

Every hotel in Melbourne was screened by picked detectives. In hundreds of cases the detectives struck up friendly talk over a beer with every American even remotely resembling their conception of the wanted man. Each inquiry drew a blank. The middle of May passed. Two women had been strangled, and the only hard conclusion was that 'the roaming brute with the strength of a gorilla' probably made his excursions from the Royal Park area.

Very late one night the telephone at our home rang. It was the Chief Commissioner, Alex Duncan. He was gravely troubled by the general state of alarm. The Government was tart, agitated and uneasy, he explained, and he was relieved to be assured that every detective who could be spared from essential war duties had been directed to the case.

The climax arrived two days later. Four detectives who had averaged three hours' sleep each night for the last week, and had not enjoyed one social drink throughout that time, marched into the main bar of the Royal Park Hotel, Queensberry Street, North Melbourne, about a mile from the Royal Park camp. They were Detective Frederick John (Blue) Adam, now a Detective Station-Officer, Detective Ernest Craig, now Superintendent First Class and chief of the Victorian division of the Australian Commonwealth Police Force, and Detectives Alec White and Ray Newton, both now retired.

All ordered a pot of beer. They sipped them slowly as their eyes roved over the faces of the Servicemen and civilians in the bar. One of the team was only half-way down his pot when he muttered urgently:

'Watch that fellow over there, on the opposite side of the bar. Ten feet away, that Yank. See, that one shaking salt and pepper in his stout. He could be our man. Look at the face now. See the flash around his cap. And look! He's grinning at us, now, the ape. The baby-faced bastard. Look at the pepper he's putting in his grog!'

The detective next to his muttering colleague calmly continued sipping beer and let his gaze rest on the soldier's face.

'You may be right,' he mused aloud. 'Cheeky peanut. Wonder if he knows we're police? Grinning right at us. Rubbishing us. Got strong hands, too. Worth a check right now.'

The four detectives huddled in conference at the bar. They agreed that a constable at a nearby station was the one man who could settle the point. It was less than a week since a young American soldier in this district had frenziedly attacked Misses Elliott and Hardy, yet been brazen enough to ask this constable for cigarettes. That had been the start of the trail leading to this area. So, if this constable identified the man, they would pull him in.

One detective slipped from the hotel to fetch the constable. Perhaps the soldier saw him leave and decided it was time to go. Or it could have been coincidence. Whatever the reason, he gulped his doctored drink, and swaggered out to the footpath.

He was still standing at the kerb, balancing lightly on his toes, as the three detectives continued their watch. Before long their colleague returned with a local constable.

'That American soldier, there,' one of the detectives whispered. 'Isn't that our man? Isn't that "The Mad Yank," the man you saw that night?'

The constable looked at the soldier for almost half a minute. Then he turned to the four expectant detectives and shook his head.

'Well, it looks like him,' he said. 'Yes, it looks like him. But it isn't. No. No, it's not our man.'

The detectives cursed.

They turned away. The soldier stepped springily on to the wet and shiny highway, threaded through the charcoal-burning cars, and was quickly gone in search of another pub.

Pretty Gladys Lilian Hosking lived nearby. Fate had chosen her to be almost torn to pieces before she died that very night!

* * *

The draughty corridors of the old bluestone Russell Street headquarters were never gloomier and more depressing than next morning when her twisted body was found in the slime and mud of an air-raid trench at Royal Park.

This was the wording of the official circular, the last of a grim series, flashed immediately to the twenty-five hundred police then in Victoria, and to all chiefs interstate:

'Superintendent's Office, Criminal Investigation Branch. Murder. – About 7 a.m. on Tuesday, the 19th May, 1942, the body of Miss Gladys Lilian Hosking was found in the Military Camp Grounds at Royal Park just a few yards inside the fence off Gatehouse Street, Parkville, by a master butcher named Albert Edgar Whiteway, of 91, Epsom Road, Ascot Vale, and a soldier named Donald Wallace McLeod, of Royal Park, and reported to the Royal Park police.

'Miss Hosking was a single woman residing at 140, Park Street, Parkville, and was employed at the Chemistry Department as secretary and librarian at Melbourne University. She left her place of employment at 6.30 p.m. supposedly for her home.

'When the body was found it was lying face downwards in mud surrounding trenches in the military grounds. It was partly clothed. The top coat and costume coat were off and lying nearby. Her purse with £4–10–0 in notes, bank book and private papers were near the body and covered in mud. Her umbrella was found still open, together with a *Herald* and a *Women's Weekly*, on the grass lawn between the roadway and the fence railing in Gatehouse Street; and a few feet away were her hat and a pair of gloves.

'The spot where these were found showed signs that the deceased had put up a struggle with her assailant, and from the position of the body it appeared as though she had been carried and dumped in the mud where she was found.

'Miss Hosking is a native of West Australia, but had been employed in various positions in Victoria for some years. Her mother is the licensee of the Railway Hotel, Hackering, West Australia. Deceased had lived at 140, Park Street, Parkville, for about twelve months, but frequently did not return home for tea at night and visited various cafés.

'She left Miss Dorothy Pettigrew at 6.30 p.m. on Monday, the 18th May, but did not state where she was going. Miss Pettigrew states that when deceased locked the door at the Chemistry Department at Melbourne University, she walked towards Sydney Road, and Miss Pettigrew towards Swanston Street, for her tram.

'It is requested that any information regarding the movements of Miss Hosking on the night of Monday the 18th of May be forthwith conveyed to the Superintendent of the CI Branch.

'About 9 p.m., Private Noel Lindsay Seymour, on special picket duty, saw an American soldier on the lawn in Gatehouse Street not far from the scene of the crime. Seymour says he was covered in mud and asked where to catch a tram to Royal Park. He said he came from Camp Pell, which is at Royal Park.

'Seymour states the man is about twenty-four years, five foot ten to eleven inches, fair and inclined-blond hair, round face, wearing American uniform. But the correct dress is not known, although he says he may be wearing a forage type of cap.

'This man may be the offender.

'R. J. Dower, Superintendent, Criminal Investigation Branch.'

Events raced towards a dramatic conclusion when the circulars went out.

It was May 20. 'The Cat' entered 'The Mad Yank' case that day. Thousands of Servicemen in every camp in and around the city were paraded that rainy day while police with umbrellas slowly reviewed their ranks. Detective Craig was among one detective squad which rushed to Port Melbourne piers when told that seven hundred American soldiers from Camp Pell had embarked there in a Matson liner and were due to leave for the New Guinea front.

They took with them the few witnesses who claimed to have seen 'Baby-face' in the Royal Park zone. Every soldier was brought on deck and screened. Many were questioned. None was the wanted man. The detective team returned to Royal Park with their witnesses to find that the massive line-ups there had also failed to produce the wanted man.

The Americans had stood there in damp, dispirited, khaki ranks for hours as thirty men and women squelched up and down the muddy camp roads and over the greasy pebbles and dank grass, anxiously searching the sea of blank, puzzled, sullen faces.

The witnesses shook their heads. The companies were dismissed. The high-ranking provost officers were grave. The police were grim. And all were glum because they feared they were again facing defeat.

By this stage they had scanned every available American in a State as big as the British Isles. Mercilessly they had dug out every Australian falsely wearing GI uniform to escape the call-to-arms or to enhance his chances with women. And the mystery, now almost overshadowing the war effort and the crisis in the north, remained the ugly and mocking question mark it had been the night Ivy McLeod had been strangled.

It was a dreary winter in 1942. Stinging rain fell again throughout the afternoon of that big search day in May. A raw wind was whining. Slowly the police detachment at Camp Pell drifted away in tiny knots to explore the remaining slim hopes.

One small group, up to their knees in mud, had solemnly been busy at the slit trench not far away. It comprised Taylor, Detective-Sergeant Frank (Tiger) Lyon, and Detective (now Detective-Inspector) William Wall Warner Mooney.

They had examined an area of mustard-yellow clay and earth around the trench where the body was found.

'The yellow clay covered an area of about four yards by three and existed between the two mounds of earth that had been removed from the trenches, and formed a V formation,'

Taylor recalled. 'The surface was very wet and adhesive and recent rain had washed the yellow clay evenly over this area.

'The trench showed a surface soil that was black, a sub-soil of a chocolate colour, and, about two feet down, the mustard-yellow clay stratum started. This was the last earth removed from the trench, and it had been thrown out so that it covered all the other earth previously removed from the trench.'

At police headquarters Taylor inspected clothing taken from Miss Hosking's body. Every item was heavily mudstained and caked with yellow clay.

That was about the stage Taylor had reached when he walked across the sodden turf towards the detectives who had been watching those big line-ups drifting away from the parade grounds of Camp Pell.

By now, some of the detectives were in the nearby rooms of the US provost officers. About four remained outside with a man who claimed rightly that he had seen this 'mad American' trying to strangle a girl at his house one night. He was one of the last witnesses remaining on the spot that cheerless day.

The jaded detectives and the civilian were lounging against a rail. It was a white rail of a simple wooden fence surrounding the Americans' sports pavilion. A few GIs were still gathered in small groups nearby. One passed carrying a pail. Another clattered down some office steps on a mission for his chief. It was a typical army scene near dusk, but one a few will never forget.

Detective Ernest Craig, next to the civilian witness, suddenly felt his right arm being gripped tightly. There was a high note of urgency in the man's hushed voice, he recalls, as he spoke.

'Eh! Eh! Eh! Eh!' The man was almost choking on his words as he shook the detective's arm. 'Ssssshhh! But yes! Yes!'

Craig looked at him sharply and saw the man nod towards a GI swinging across the oval.

'That's him!' the man almost hissed. 'Him. Yes, *him*!'

'What? Baby-face? You're sure?' said Craig.

'Dead right! Not a doubt in the world,' the man insisted.

Someone ran to the provost's office. Someone else ordered out the guard. There was the drumming of boots and the scraping of steel on steel. The American halted in his tracks, and looked round at an encircling fence of Thompson sub-machine-guns. His name was Edward Joseph Leonski. He was the grinning Yank seen pouring pepper in his drink at the Parkville pub two days before.

He was the only soldier who had been able to avoid identification in the mass parades of the past few days. How he missed parades, and had his absence from them covered, was a puzzle at the time. It is as big a mystery still, and never will be explained.

* * *

Under the strongest suspicion, but still with no indictable evidence against him, Leonski was locked inside a high compound while Taylor and some detectives went to the tent he had shared with other men.

When Taylor had been down at the slit trench he had noticed that marks in the yellow mud must have been made by clawing hands and skidding feet.

Now, as he was about to enter Leonski's tent, he went through the normal movements of a man sweeping back the heavy flap from outside. He stepped through the opening. His hand went across and slightly up the inswept canvas. There, at the very spot where his hand was resting as the heavy canvas was held back, was hardened mustard-yellow mud.

It was mud transferred there by a hand.

Taylor noticed then that the army issue comforter, or counterpane, was missing from Leonski's bed. Maybe it had been washed, in which case any tell-tale mud would be missing from it. The patch found on the tent fly was important, but alone it was not enough to identify or brand a murderer. It could have been left by another man.

Taylor's eyes roved the roomy tent that held four men, and his mind darted back to his field days as a mining assayer, when he had slept more often under canvas than a roof. He lowered himself to the edge of Leonski's stretcher.

As he had expected, he found that, to prevent himself sinking and falling back against the tent's wall canvas, he had had to grip the sides of the stretcher with both hands, one extended each side of his body. But he was careful to place those hands a little wider apart than usual. For there on the under surface of the stretcher's side rib were fingerprints in drying mustard-yellow mud.

The missing comforter was found. It had been sent to be laundered. On one side was a patch of the persistent mustard-colour mud.

This was enough to warrant the immediate interrogation of Leonski. Some of the salient points, taken from the original record of that day, were:

What is your name? – Edward Joseph Leonski.

We are from the Police Department. I am Detective-Sergeant McGuffie. This is Detective-Sergeant Lyon, and this is Detective Murray (shorthand writer). You know your officers (present), Lieutenant Johnstone and Corporal Zorfas? – Yes.

Are these your shoes? – Yes. I know the rip (referring to a cut in the leather of one of the shoes).

Is this your jacket? – Yes.

Are these your trousers? – Yes.

Is this your towel? – Yes. That's right. I picked it up in the latrine one day.

And is this your towel? (referring to a towel bearing yellow mud) – It could be.

You had some singlets like these? – Yes.

There is yellow mud on this singlet. How do you suggest you got yellow stains on your jacket and this singlet? – I do not know if this is my singlet. I might have got it walking around near the kitchen.

I suggest to you this is yellow mud. Where did you get it? – I might have slipped up around the tent somewhere when I was happy and good.

Are these newspapers about the murders yours? – I bought some newspapers about the murders.

The newspapers were found inside a tin found in your tent. Are they yours? – Yes, I must have stuffed them inside the tin.

Are these accessories yours? – Yes.

Can you tell us where this yellow mud came from in your towel? – Somebody else must have wiped themselves on it.

There is yellow mud on your shoes. How do you account

for that? – There must be yellow mud near my tent. So far as I can say there is no such mud there.

Were you in any other part of Camp Pell on the night of the 18th of this month? – When I have been drinking I forget where I have been.

Detective-Sergeant McGuffie then asked Leonski if he knew of Gatehouse Street, Parkville, and Leonski insisted that his only knowledge of that district came from newspaper reading. He insisted that he had no recollection of having been there during the Monday night after he left the hotel. But McGuffie pressed hard. He rearranged the red carnation he usually wore in his buttonhole and went on with his questions.

Will you say you were *not* in Gatehouse Street before returning to the camp? – I cannot remember being there.

Is it possible that you have forgotten? – From what my friends tell me, it is possible. I do not always remember where I have been when I am drunk. My friends tell me that they have seen this place and that place and I don't remember.

Are you responsible for your actions when you are drunk? – Yes.

Do you claim responsibility for anything you have done since you have been in Australia at least? – Yes.

Do you always understand the consequences of your acts? – OK. I have always had that idea, anyhow.

On Monday night last, the 18th of this month, a woman lost her life in Camp Pell and it is in consequence of that woman losing her life that you are being questioned here today. – Yes, I understand that.

Did you go down to the spot where the woman's body was found? – No, I was washing clothes.

Will you say you have never been near the spot where that woman's body was found? – I could have been near the spot after leaving the hotel.

Could you have been in Camp Pell near the spot without remembering it? – Yes.

Is it possible to have been near the spot where that woman was murdered? – Yes, that is possible. I might have been.

You have molested women on other occasions in Parkville and you always laugh when you do. – No answer.

On the 12th of this month, a young woman was walking along Wimble Street, Parkville. She was accosted by a soldier who asked could he walk along with her. She said she could not very well stop him. He walked along with her until she reached her gate and he then caught her by the throat. The description of the soldier fits you, and I have no hesitation in saying that in an identification parade she will pick you. – I contradict that. It is silly. It is not true.

On the 14th of this month a young woman was walking along Gatehouse Street and entered the door of her home. You pushed in behind her (here, for the first time, the squat, broad McGuffie sternly points an accusing finger) and you followed her into the kitchen of her home and there you were met by her uncle. You have been positively identified by him. – I have never seen that man before in my life!

What do you say to that? – I have no recollection of trailing any girl into a house or meeting her uncle.

Do you say you were not in Camp Pell near where that woman's body was found on Monday night? – I don't know. How far is it from the hotel? I might have passed that area.

Did you fall in the mud down there? – I fell somewhere that night, but I don't remember where.

Have you ever had any conversation regarding any other murder with any other person? – I know that point. It is too easy. I have always worried (Private) Gallo. Nobody can fathom him. He always thought that I was bad. I wanted to shock him. When the captain came into the guard tent to ask me if I was guilty or not guilty, I saw a statement in his hand – Private J. Gallo. I knew that was Gallo's statement. I saw the first few lines when the captain had it. I told Gallo I had done these murders. It might have been one or two.

Did you tell him how you did them? – Yes, I guess I told him I strangled them. I was sprung when I told him.

Did you tell him you had got money from these women you had murdered? – I don't remember that.

Will you deny you told him about the money? – I think I told him about some money – a pound and a half.

Did you show him some Australian cigarettes and tell him you got them from the girl you had murdered? – No, I don't remember that.

Did you tell him that you had got a pound and a half? – Yes, something like that.

Did you buy newspapers regarding these murders and keep them? – Yes, so that I could keep up with the murders and tell Gallo.

McGuffie, then the elder statesman of the homicide squad, cleared his throat and read Private Anthony J. Gallo's statement. Leonski shouted a denial. McGuffie went on with the questioning.

Is it a coincidence that you told him you murdered these women, and that you were seen in the park near where this last girl was murdered all covered with yellow mud, and the murdered girl was all covered with yellow mud? – How do you know this girl was murdered there and not carried from somewhere else?

What do you say about the park now? – I might have been in that part of the park. I don't remember being in that part of the park. People tell me about seeing this place and that place and I never remember being there.

Have you ever been in trouble back home? – I was charged with rape in San Antonio. I cannot remember when it was. Oh, a long time ago. About a year, I guess.

How do you account for this yellow mud? (showing the bed counterpane to him) – Private Carlson did that. He was drunk in my tent that day and put his boots on my cover. He did that.

When? – About Sunday.

Where had he been before he came to your tent? – We had been out drinking.

Where had he been prior to lying on your bed? – I don't know where he got that yellow mud.

I would expect to find black mud – not yellow – as the mud around your tent is black. Would you not expect to find black mud and not yellow mud on his boots? – If he had been in any area where that yellow mud was, he would get it on his boots.

Is that the only class of mud that you had on your clothes? – I did not pay much attention.

Can you show us the spot where you fell over? – I am not sure where I fell.

There is yellow mud on the entrance to your tent that was not there three or four days before. – A lot of soldiers come over to see their friends, and they might have brought it there.

Can you say who came there with yellow mud on them? – I cannot remember any person who was there with yellow mud on them.

Where were you on Monday afternoon? – I had been to the Parkville Hotel and drank there until they closed.

Were you sober? – I was feeling pretty good.

When you entered the camp, where did you go first? – I went to the latrine and then went back to my tent.

What did you do when you got into your tent? – Took off my clothes and got into bed.

Leonski was then taken to Royal Parade, Parkville, where McGuffie asked him: 'Can you point out the house you were in after leaving the hotel?'

Leonski was not certain. He said he could swear only that it was a house with a room that had four beds in it.

As they walked back to camp, McGuffie stopped abruptly at the corner of Royal Parade and Park Street. He said accusingly to Leonski: 'You were seen right here about seven o'clock on Monday night, talking to a woman who had an umbrella up!'

'It could not have been me!' Leonski almost screamed. 'It was *not* me!'

* * *

Throughout the orderly well-marshalled interrogation Leonski had kept his head. But it must have registered, even in his peculiar mind, that whether he cracked or not the police and Taylor intended to make the mud the fulcrum on which their case hinged.

Here is Taylor's official version of his faith in that mustard-colour mud at that tense time, although the strong reasons for it were not revealed until later:

'I inspected a tent in the US military camp. There were four beds in this tent. One bed was said to be used by a soldier named Leonski. On this bed, about midway along its length, two decided patches of mustard-yellow clay existed on the side angle frame of this bed, suggesting that a person sat on the bed and touched the places with mud-stained hands.

'On a quilt, or comforter, I found a large yellow mudstain about seven inches by four inches centrally on this article. The tent itself showed four yellow mudstains above the bed in four separate places on the inside of the fabric.

'At the entrance to the tent, on the right side entering from the north, a large yellow mudstain existed on the outside of the tent fabric. This stain had been partly washed down by rain. All these tent and bed stains were made by mustard-yellow clay similar in colour and in constitution to the yellow clay existing where Hosking's body had been found.

'The surface soil where the tent was pitched was black. I examined a soldier's jacket which had been washed and was still wet. A trace of yellow mud existed on the outside near the left sleeve opening at the wrist. A pair of trousers, washed and still wet, contained a few grains of sand inside the right side pocket.

'A few grains of this sand were iron-stained. Similar iron-stained sand existed in this clay.

'I examined a pair of tan shoes containing the figures 590 stamped on the soles inside. I found mustard-yellow clay adhering to the soles in front of the heels of the shoes. Surface clay had been washed off, showing particles embedded in the remaining clay. Yellow clay existed in the eyelet holes. Traces of yellow clay existed also inside both shoes near the top.

'Traces of yellow clay existed along the stitching midway down the shoes between the eyelet holes. Traces of yellow clay existed also inside both shoes under the tongue. One shoe was cut through the upper at the large toe joint for about one inch in length.

'A singlet had yellow mudstains on both sleeves from the wrist to the elbow and also on the bottom edge. A small patch of mud existed centrally.

'This clothing was said to be the property of Edward Joseph

Leonski. A Turf cigarette cardboard packet, a water bottle and a *Herald* newspaper dated 18/5/42 were stained with yellow mud.

'I examined earth around an electric light pole near a wash-house in the US camp at Royal Park, also earth along a drainage line running south-east from a shower house and around a hydrant on a pipe-line in this locality. I found that these areas contained earth coloured black, dark brown, cocoa colour and light yellow – all in small patches.

'I could find no patches of light yellow clay in these areas greater than two feet across, and these existed near the hydrant and electric light poles only. Generally, the earth was in similar patches as would result from the variously coloured layers being mixed up in the refilling of the pipe-lines and the post-holes.'

In brief, experiment and comparison had convinced Taylor that the mud and earth near the kitchen, where Leonski had said he 'might have slipped,' was not identical in colour and components with the soil and the clay around the slit trench where the body had been found.

Taylor was prepared to swear on oath that, even if all the samples of mud had been identical, they did not exist in such quantity inside the camp to have plastered Leonski so liberally.

'Baby-face' was interviewed again.

He was confronted in the Camp Pell military police office by Detective F. J. Adam, Detective W. W. W. Mooney, Detective Murray, the US camp adjutant, Captain Wayne Bailey, Captain Servis, and Lieutenant Johnstone. Adam, like Mooney, was born to make murder investigation a career, and to man a periscope on the underworld for three decades. He is one of the world's veteran manhunters. Even a quarter of a century ago he had scores of notches on his homicide baton.

That day Adam came quite bluntly to the point.

He reminded 'Baby-face' – and Adam had deep distaste for this particular type of baby face – that only one hour earlier that afternoon an Australian soldier had sworn to having seen Leonski early in the night of May 18.

'You were then covered with yellow mud, Leonski,' Adam said. He said it as though the words came from a voice box that had lost its sense of tone. 'And you were then near the spot where Miss Hosking's body was found.'

Leonski hung his head for some time. When he raised it he asked: 'What is my position if it is proved that I killed the girl? Will the army deal with me, or will I be handed over to the civil police?'

Captain Servis said: 'That is a matter that will be left to the American Army authorities. It is for them to decide. But I think that the army will deal with it.'

'Leonski was quiet for about half a minute,' Adam said later. 'He then put his head in his hands, and said: "I choked her." '

'Then tell us,' Adam pursued, 'just what happened.'

Leonski's three confessions describing the murders of Ivy McLeod, Pauline Thompson, and Gladys Hosking then came tumbling from him.

'Baby-face, the Mad Yank,' was charged at the city watch-house opposite Russell Street headquarters, on the crest of the windy hill where I write.

Captain Servis had been correct. The US Army did ask the right to deal with the prisoner.

Envoys from the US Army arrived at Detective-Superintendent Dower's office at headquarters right opposite the lodge hall – now demolished – where Leonski would later be tried. They recognised the sovereignty of the State, they said, but asked for the live body so that justice could be served by his countrymen.

The Chief Secretary's Department and the Police Department agreed to trial by American court-martial on the readily accepted conditions that the accused be kept in strict custody on police premises and that police evidence be tendered at his trial.

The next day, May 23, 1942, through APO 501, Headquarters of the United States Army Forces in Australia issued restricted Special Orders No. 129, announcing 'A general court-martial is appointed to meet at this headquarters for the trial of such persons as may be properly brought before it.'

* * *

The noose had settled around Leonski's neck. But could his

accusers draw it tight? Was the case truly watertight? Leonski pleaded not guilty to every charge, and alleged confessions had been repudiated, mangled and discarded in the past. Would Leonski insist, for example, that he covered himself in yellow mud by slipping in those patches near the kitchen? Could he prove that the patches at that time were bigger than the police could prove?

Not in the opinion of the Government Analyst.

Taylor stood easy but unshakable at the imposing court-martial as the usual doubts and arguments were directed up at him like a barrage.

Couldn't Leonski – or any other American, Dutchman, Filippino, Australian, New Zealander or Britisher in the town – have got that mud on him almost anywhere, almost any time, during these past few weeks?

No, said 'The Cat' implacably.

Why was that?

In his reply Taylor took the facts in order. First, Gladys Hosking had died at Royal Park, an area which happened to be an ancient fossil zone, where the layers of earth were quite distinctive from those in other parts of Melbourne.

Second, the soil at this park area consisted of a top layer of black earth, a layer of grey clay, one of yellow ochre, and deeper a fourth layer of ironstone gravel or what is described as infiltrated salicious stone.

Third, the layers in the mounds of soil around that slit trench lay in reverse order – the order in which they had been dug out. That is, the ironstone gravel and the yellow ochre were spreadeagled on the top, and the grey clay and black earth well underneath.

The defence pointed out that, away from this trench and nearer the US camp, workmen had recently laid pipes in similar earth – that is, right in the same belt of this peculiar fossil zone.

Taylor agreed.

The defence thereupon argued that Leonski could easily have plastered himself with this yellow ochre mud and infiltrated salicious gravel on these filled-in excavations while returning, perhaps unsteadily, back to camp one night.

'The Cat' shook his head several times. No, he said, there wasn't a possible chance of that. Because that pipe-line track had been quite shallow. The lower layers of soil – that is, the mustard-yellow ochre and the ironstone gravel stratum – had *not* been disturbed by the diggers. The little bits of yellow clay that may have been found there were not from those underlying layers. They were just pieces of ordinary clay from the top soil layers, as might be found in any garden.

If any further proof were needed, Taylor allowed these indisputable scientific and geological facts make their point:

Yellow ochre commercial paint was made from mustard-colour mud like that found at the Hosking trench. There were other places in the Victorian countryside – notably the volcanic region of the Western District – where similar mud existed, but with one big difference – it was clear. It did not contain any of the tiny gravel that he had found at the Hosking trench. That was why the yellow mud in this fossil zone had not been and never would be commercially exploited to make yellow ochre paint. It was why the belt had seldom been disturbed until the war came along. The cost of removing that tiny gravel would have been exorbitant.

The tiny gravel in the yellow mud at the Hosking trench, however, was identical with the tiny gravel Taylor had found in the yellow mud on Leonski's clothes and on the insteps of the shoes the American had tried desperately to clean.

Leonski's doom was sealed.

He was found guilty and sentenced to death. The decision was unanimous and was, under the American 48th Article of War, confirmed by President Franklin D. Roosevelt.

Leonski is believed to have been the only convicted murderer of any race to be held in custody in the cells of the Melbourne city watch-house opposite police headquarters.

For long weeks he played softball against the walls that had been torn at frantically and forlornly by thousands of derelicts, drunks and demented men. He read the life of Ned Kelly there. He drew figures of soft women with transparent drapes. Sometimes he crooned soothingly, or scribbled rhymes that never rose above the level of doggerel. Always he was pleasant to those who took him his meals. Often he walked on the hands that so easily had crushed life out. He never failed each morning to take his exercise by walking briskly up and down the long, cold flagged corridors and turning hand springs or catherine wheels.

His watch-house keepers told me he was very nimble and surprisingly athletic. Until the morning of his execution he proclaimed to them his faith in physical fitness.

On the morning of November 9, 1942 – after his sentence had been ratified in Washington – he was escorted by US provost troops to an army prison van parked outside the watch-house. It was all over in about half an hour. The van was driven non-stop three miles to Pentridge Gaol, a grim, blue-stone penitentiary once known as 'The Stockade' when built by criminal labour during the roaring goldfield days more than a century ago. The executioner was waiting by the gallows, the same beam, trap and lever once used at the old Melbourne Gaol for the executions of Ned Kelly, Richard Deeming, Martha Needle, Arnold Sodeman, Angus Murray, Colin Ross, and an army of other murderers.

Leonski's remains were interred in the garden of the Spring-vale Crematorium, ten miles from Melbourne. He was buried away from the small graves of his countrymen who had not tarnished their nation's honour.

No flower was planted above this grave. But his casket was among those later disinterred and removed to New Guinea on the first leg back home when the war had ended and all warriors were allowed to rest.

There the trail gives out. No word came back. But perhaps the remains were received by his sister in America, the one known to have wept when told her brother had been hanged, and who cried in her grief: 'But it can't be our Eddie! He was always so kind, always so gentle.'

9 Cat and Colossus

TAYLOR always had a puckish sense of humour. It carried him through refreshingly on macabre assignments and during gruelling days when the truth was particularly evasive. But seldom did he need it more than the morning in 1946 when he confronted a battered and heavily soldered square kerosene drum among the many pots and cans marked for his immediate attention. His frown deepened as he read the label on the drum and methodically ripped up the soldered lid with a kitchen can opener.

Just as the label said, the drum was packed tightly with something that could have been a number of enormous motor tyre tubes or a deflated and compressed dirigible. It was neither. Here was quite the rarest, oddest and possibly most grotesque of all strange things he had been persuaded to examine.

'It was pale pink,' says Taylor, 'and when it was unravelled from the tin it was almost big enough to fill a car.'

He reached for his rubber gloves and spread the strange specimen across the linoleumed floor of his cluttered office. Then he stood staring down at – an elephant's stomach!

It had come from a huge and valuable African elephant which had been the pride of Wirth's Circus, then touring the district of Numurkah, an agricultural township in the Goulburn Valley, near the north border of Victoria.

An accompanying letter was from the local police. They

said the elephant was well the night before it was found dead. It had eaten chaff and straw at sundown, but was dead at its tethering post when its keeper took out a morning snack next day. The circus troupe were convinced their prize animal had been poisoned maliciously, and the police had found no reason to disagree with them. But there was no apparent motive for poisoning a colossus that had not annoyed anyone by trumpeting and, in any case, had been tethered too far from the township to have been a nuisance to those living there.

Taylor wondered if this was the first evidence that someone was working off a grudge and whether other costly animals might be killed. Perhaps the elephant was only the first target. According to the letter it had been hitched on an open patch many yards from tents and cages. A highly dangerous situation would have been set up here, because someone who did not know the vulnerability of some animals to certain poisons probably would have used a vast amount to kill one this size.

'The elephant had cost at least £500, probably the equivalent of £2,000 today,' Taylor told me. 'The Wirth company had good enough reason to complain about the financial loss and the effect the death of the elephant would have on their tour. But their real fear was for the security of dangerous and valuable tigers and other savage beasts.

'Once humans with hidden motives attack imprisoned jungle animals, who can say they will not free the lot in a moment of madness? My first steps were to determine if poison actually had been used. The hidden danger was that a poisoner inexperienced in dosages could fail to kill, but could torment and enrage wild beasts to an alarming danger level.'

When Taylor examined his extraordinary exhibit he found angry scarlet marks on the stomach walls. Some were almost four inches square. Others were the size of a sixpence. But scores were only the size of match heads, and there was a number no larger than pinheads or specks of dust. It was the range of smaller marks that attracted Taylor's eye before he turned his attentions to the contents of the stomach.

He found chaff, straw, traces of water, apples, salt, a little earth and gravel – the combination one would expect to find in the stomach of a healthy, non-carnivorous animal.

But there was an exception. One thing was missing, and that, to 'The Cat's' keen eyes and razor-sharp reasoning, was most intriguing. In fact, it might be vital. It could be the basis of all reasoning in this case. Tests were not needed to convince him that the elephant had died through arsenical poisoning. The angry, flaming red patches were completely characteristic and conclusive to him. But, in case it were disputed later, Taylor made laboratory tests which confirmed his observations.

He rang the Numurkah police. Crackling over the long-distance wire came the answer he had expected. He was assured no one had been allowed to tamper with the stomach. Nothing was removed or changed and nothing had been washed away. The stomach was exactly as a puzzled and perspiring country doctor had cut it out for dispatch to the crime chemist.

Taylor rang off and then wrote down the ingredient missing from the stomach contents – common, ordinary grass.

He listed these points:

He had the stomach of an animal, with a prodigious appetite, that had been tethered in the open for many hours, if not days. It had not been sick before it ate for the last time. On the contrary, from tests and appearance the elephant was in its prime. Yet there was no evidence that even a microscopic speck of grass had been sucked in by a powerful elephant that, like all his kind, liked to snuffle, if not graze.

The Numurkah police shortly afterwards confirmed the reason why there was no evidence of grass. It was simply that no grass was growing in the gravelly patch around the elephant's hitching post.

Every particle of food the elephant had eaten had been hand fed to it, and every keeper and attendant known to have been in contact with the animal was considered to be beyond suspicion.

'Of course there isn't any grass,' Taylor agreed over the phone. 'I'm not rebuffed by that. Had there been any grass I would have found evidence of it here. But why is there no grass near that tent? There's plenty of it in other places around Numurkah, isn't there?'

The policeman at the other end of the line quickly vouched for the locality's fertility.

'Tell me, if you know, why there's no grass near that tent,' Taylor demanded.

'I haven't got a clue,' the policeman many miles distant admitted. 'Maybe the kids have been playing football there and worn it bare. Maybe it was burned out somehow.'

'Well, do this,' Taylor told him. 'Go to every farmhouse, hotel or shanty pub in your district. Establish just how many strangers – tourists, travellers, thieves, anyone – have been in or near your district over the past few months. In fact, check back for two years if you can. Let me know when they were there and for how long. Also what did they do? Where did they go? What did they buy or what did they sell? Make the check as thorough as you can.'

It was a tall order. But the policeman – one of those incomparable Australian outback police who command territory bigger than a general might direct in war – promised to do his best.

No station or occurrence books of any police post in the world hold records of every stranger who comes to town. Only those who have come under notice for violation or suspicion have their names and movements taken down. But there are other ways and means of checking strangers in every Australian town where news travels fast because it is a rare commodity, and where the movements of strangers are recorded in inquisitive rural minds.

The constable was back on the phone later in the week with a remarkably comprehensive list. Taylor was ruthlessly selective as the policeman reeled it off.

'Out,' he grunted as the names were called out. 'No apparent connection there. Don't worry about that party. No, I don't think so. Not a possibility there. No. No. What was that again?' he asked quickly. 'Tell me everything you know about this little group that came to town.'

When Taylor had finished making his notes, he drew hard on another cigarette and said: 'Just one more question to wind up this odd case. The circus came to town on the fourth of the month. But the elephant was dead next day? Very well, I'll give you the answer shortly.'

In his personal diary he wrote that day: 'This is the case of the elephant I'll not forget.' His pen continued scratching this report:

'Positively, the death was not malicious. This animal died violently from arsenical poisoning, but there is no cause for alarm. The fatal dose was self-administered under rather wry circumstances.

'An elephant is a vegetable eater. For this reason, its stomach is more soluble and sensitive to arsenic than that of meat-eating man. Arsenic stops the work of the blood, is durable, and does not decay. Arsenic can kill any living thing, including an elephant or a whale. Those are chemical facts. The next logical facts from effect to cause are drawn from natural history.

'A horse, like a dog, is fond of rolling and gambolling in the grass or dust. A budgerigar, even in a cage, will dust its wings to rid itself of insects. And a two-ton elephant likes to blast its huge form with, say, gravel. It scoops it up with its trunk and showers it over its chest and back to give itself much the same vibratory pleasure that a human derives from a massage.

'This elephant did just that. When he was enjoying this practice some of the gravel was blown into his mouth. He swallowed many stones, some quite tiny, others the size of a pea. Yet five times that amount of ordinary stones and gravel would not have affected the animal's health and digestion except that, in this case, every one of those stones was coated liberally with arsenic.

'Despite its proud and justifiable claim to fertility, Numurkah suffers from a plague of weeds. As the local policeman established, months before the elephant died two travelling salesmen had come to town. They camped outside the town and invited local farmers to see "a remarkable demonstration." On the very spot where, about a year later, Wirth's were to tether their enormous elephant, they carried out this demonstration.

'The Numurkah police established that the salesmen poured and sprayed the contents of many bottles on the ground. The liquid covered a fairly wide area of weeds and natural grass growing in a soil well studded with pebbles and gravel. They announced they had the most effective destroyer of any known weed, and guaranteed it to be absolutely harmless to all but unwanted plant life.

'Next day the weeds had died, and the next year, when the famous circus arrived in town, death claimed its mammoth elephant.'

When he discussed the case with me Taylor concluded wryly:

'As I said, arsenic is durable. It goes on and on. So do shyster salesmen.'

10 Death aboard the 'Samarkand'

Death Aboard the 'Samarkand' could easily be the title of a thriller, transporting the reader with armchair ease to the ironbound coast of Africa or the steely blue of the China Sea. Or perhaps projecting mental flashes of the hordes of Jenghiz Khan surging through the valley of the Sogd and crowning his butcheries with the bloodbath of ancient Samarkand.

At least, it is doubtful whether one would identify such a title with a drama played nervously in Victoria's wind-beaten port of Geelong in 1945, when four British seamen died, several came perilously close to death, and others were saved only by the quick senses of the unassuming but uncannily perceptive 'Cat.'

As with several of his other triumphs, his work on this case was not given the public acclaim it deserved. The court report on his evidence was dull and scanty, reduced to a few uninformative paragraphs in a provincial newspaper.

But it was responsible for the British Board of Admiralty, acting on the advice of an Australian Director of Navigation, Captain J. O. Davis, CBE, radioing urgent warnings and strict orders to every ship under the Red Duster. Britain was determined to ensure that seamen's lives were never lost the same way again.

The case also prompted an Australian coroner to say in court: 'I was inspired by Mr Taylor's evidence and accepted it as giving the correct cause. We have no evidence of a similar fatality.'

The *Samarkand* was a typical liberty ship, one of the thousands turned out, night and day, in a hundred shipyards of the world to balance the disastrous losses inflicted by German U-boat packs. Her number was 169715. She was registered in London and owned by Alfred Holt and Co. She was of 7,219 tons gross and was built in America in 1943 for the British Government for what is styled 'bare boat charter.'

She was tired when her war ended. She had tramped every ocean, often alone, rarely in convoy, dodging submarines, nervously preferring mid-ocean routes, and shy always of marauding, land-based aircraft. Taking into account the war's misfortunes and frustrations, it seems that she was a happy enough ship with a crew well shaken down, and justifiably proud of their shuttle service of mixed cargoes to any vital point of the Allied fronts.

She burned oil, fed to the furnaces through pipes that passed through her dark, forty-foot-deep ironclad holds, which were never pierced by torpedoes, yet suddenly held death firmly and fiendishly as soon as the crew's most perilous days of war had passed.

None could dub her a wanton or fickle ship. She had done her duty many times and never failed her master or his men.

Uneventfully at Montreal, in 1945, she took aboard a cargo of Canadian wheat, delivered it to Holland, and went in ballast to Bone, in Algeria, near the frontier of Tunisia. Australian farmers were then desperately short of superphosphate fertiliser for the wheat belts along the southern and eastern continental strips. The Pacific island of Nauru, for so long their main source of fertilisers, had been blasted out of action by the Japanese. For three years Australian farmers had been dependent almost entirely on supplies sneaked in from overseas. So, at Bone, the *Samarkand's* holds were packed with phosphatic rock to be crushed and treated in Australian phosphate mills.

The ship was well trimmed. The cargo did not shift. She reached Fremantle safely in August, 1945. And when she berthed on the 20th at Cresco Quay, Geelong, the world was basking in relief and celebrating final victory in the Pacific zone. There were no threats of waterfront disputes or other possible hitches in unloading.

Her scheduled stay in port was brief. But as they exchanged the usual badinage with waterside workers the crew looked forward to a quick stretch ashore. The chief officer and a young apprentice at his heels were among them. But there were shipboard tasks to be attended to before any could hope to reach Geelong, or Melbourne, more than forty miles beyond.

Captain Peter Dunsire was the *Samarkand's* master. He had been at sea for thirty years and was acknowledged to be a most dependable master mariner. But the legitimate and regulation orders he had passed about eight bells in the morning watch – 8 a.m. – were soon to lead, as later he officially reported, 'to circumstances he had never experienced before.'

These orders included the opening and thorough inspection of certain ballast tanks that had been dry and empty for about three months.

The captain had specifically ordered his chief officer, William Archibald Jones, of London, a seaman of sixteen years' experience, to unseal the deep tanks in the after part of the ship.

The records of the Navigation Department and the coroner quote Captain Dunsire as saying: 'There were four similar tanks in the forward part of the ship and two aft. I had told Mr Jones to open the aft tanks, but the forward tanks (of holds number 1 and 2) were opened unknown to me. But Mr Jones was a very experienced first mate, and although I had given no specific instructions for the forward tanks to be opened, he had power to do so.'

Captain Dunsire also put on record that Jones was 'a very exacting and trustworthy officer' and that three other men who were about to die were also experienced and reliable seamen. They were Christopher Ewbank, of Manchester, a sea cadet with nearly four years' unblemished sea service to his credit, Third Officer William Diggin la Touche Balden, of Blackpool, a man of many parts whose serious studies included art, music, meteorology, and George Powell Worsp, of Liverpool, chief steward and first aid officer who had been at sea for twenty years and, as his captain testified, 'was always on duty in the event of an accident.'

But now their talents and their devotion to duty were to be annihilated by a devilish enemy they could not feel or see.

Somewhere about 9 a.m., Chief Officer Jones, with torch in hand, went down into No. 1 hold with Cadet Chris Ewbank. They clambered thirty feet down the narrow, vertical steel ladders into sheer blackness split only by the flashlight's feeble beam, and took a few groping steps along a steel platform, and then climbed ten feet down another ladder to the bottom of the capacious tank.

This tank, in the forward bowels of the *Samarkand*, was more than thirty feet long and ten feet deep, and of an average width of twenty-one feet. Its walls were iron and steel plates and girders, and its capacity was about 6,600 cubic feet.

At this time, several men were on the main deck near the uncovered hatch. They included John Roy Massey, a senior midshipman, senior ordinary seamen Cedric Hingley Parsons and John Watson, who were removing bolts and tightening nuts, John Saunders, the ship's engineer, Ronald Baxter, a seaman, Cadets Rex Stein and James Murphy, Arthur Clutterbuck, a stevedore, of Corio Street, Geelong, and his foreman, William Spedding.

None who saw the two seamen disappear below had more than a passing interest in their task. It was a routine duty, an affair of only a few minutes for a skilled chief officer and a competent sea cadet.

Seaman John Watson saw Jones clamber down towards the bottom of the hatch, shine his torch into the tank on the port side, and then heard him begin to grope his way into the starboard side tank.

'Mr Jones had been down there with Ewbank a little more than five minutes when he popped his head out of a manhole and called Mr Balden down,' Seaman Watson later recalled. 'At this time Mr Balden had been working with me not far from the tank. Mr Jones and Mr Balden then went down into that tank, and there was nothing in their actions to cause alarm. I went on working, and a few minutes later Mr Balden came out and called for a heaving line. He seemed to be all right when I dropped the heaving line down. I still kept on working until I went for a smoke.'

Seaman Parsons had also heard Balden shout for the heaving line. He swore that everything appeared to be shipshape when he also went for a smoke some twenty minutes later.

About half an hour had passed since Jones and Ewbank had first gone below, followed by Balden a few minutes later. Those on deck had no misgivings at this stage. They assumed the three had found some damage in the tank and were attending to it on the spot without bothering to call for extra help.

But the continuing silence grew heavy with premonition. Officers and seamen began to crane and listen, and shouted inquiries that received no answer save echoes from black space.

Senior Midshipman John Roy thought he could make out a faint pin-prick of light below and wondered if he had indeed heard a faint call for help. He sprinted to the bridge, announced his fears to the captain, then ran to get help from a stout old former sea-dog, Bill Spedding, who was in charge of the unloading gangs.

On deck near the hatch the strained silence was broken as volunteers coughed, shuffled forward spitting on their hands, and offered to take the first rungs of the ladders that seemed to lead to unknown peril.

Massey went down with his own torch. Down went Boatswain Saunders, and Baxter, Stein and Murphy. Down went Spedding, Clutterbuck, and Chief Steward Worsp.

Saunders soon reeled up from the tank to the bottom of the hatch and collapsed. So did Worsp, Baxter, Stein and Murphy. Others fought their way back to the top of the hatch. Brave Clutterbuck lashed a rope to the unconscious Saunders, collapsed himself, gasped and struggled to the top again, then went down again to collapse once more and be hauled somehow from the closing jaws of death.

Massey managed to scramble to the top. Spedding came up, too, looking ghastly, and more dead than alive.

They had been down only forty-five seconds. But none could speak. Somehow, some had managed to lash lines to those who could not move. All those who reached the deck collapsed.

They retched and choked and waved their weakening arms. Four, unconscious and on the brink of death, were rushed by ambulance to Geelong Hospital.

They were unable to tell of Clutterbuck's valour below as he tried to drag two men to safety or to tell of the gallantry of Bill Spedding, who had heroically helped to bring them up.

Then Worsp gallantly went down again, with his first-aid gear, never to return alive.

On the *Samarkand's* main deck, as he vanished from view, a knot of men who had survived many perils of the deep heard the wheeling gulls screech a solemn requiem and wondered what mystery was locked in the ship's holds.

* * *

In distant Melbourne Charles Anthony Taylor put down the receiver of his telephone, took off his chemical-stained white coat, and stepped into a car which sped down the long connecting highway to the Corio waterfront. His face was like a frozen mask, the lips thin and tight and the eyes narrowed.

Senior Detective Philip Henry Ward, called post-haste to the ship, had confirmed that there must be four bodies closeted mysteriously in the holds. Seamen with troubled eyes were waiting anxiously and expectantly for the arrival of the Government Analyst. Several, impressed by the quiet demeanour of the bespectacled analyst, volunteered to accompany him below.

Wretched moments passed as the party, with torches flashing, crept slowly down the hatch and disappeared over the lips of the gaping ballast tank.

One man was ahead of Taylor by just a few feet. It may have been providential that he was. Taylor could see him clearly in his torch beam, and he heard him break the eerie silence for the first time since they had left the light and sounds above.

The man gave a short laugh. 'I just pitched head over heels,' he announced. 'You know, I never been able to do a somersault before.'

None could see 'The Cat's' face in the gloom. But he believes it must have registered the fear he suddenly felt, for recognition of the enormous danger confronting them all had come to him in a flash.

'Wait!' he called. 'Every one of you! Don't go any farther. Get out of this hold at once!'

On deck once more, he turned to a startled ship's officer.

'Where did you pump in your fresh-water ballast?' he demanded. 'Was it fresh or was it salt? Was it brackish? Try to remember, for the lives of your men may depend on it!'

The officer stared at Taylor, and admitted the water had been brackish.

'So,' Taylor said, 'there was salt in it. You pumped it in downriver in Holland and out at Bone? Are you sure? Because if you are right, and any of us follow, we'll die.'

'I'm right,' the officer replied uneasily. 'But what if the water ballast had been fresh?'

'In that case,' Taylor told him, 'the cause of death would be even more of a riddle than it appears now. But you are certain that it was brackish, that it contained salt?'

'I'm positive,' the officer said.

Taylor held up a hand. 'These few chips I'm holding,' he told the officer, 'will prove there's no cyanide or other deadly gas, as you possibly suspect. In fact, the truth will be much more elementary. But what I suspect is just as deadly, though I've no knowledge of it ever happening before. That brackish water was the catalysis,' he added.

Seamen were staring at Taylor as they rested against the main deck rails, limp with tension and shock.

Taylor told his listeners he had no doubt that their mates below were dead. But he added his assurance that none had suffered, and then announced that the bodies could not be removed until necessary equipment was available.

'A catalysis,' he explained briefly, 'is the decomposition of one substance by the mere presence of another, which in itself remains unchanged.' He opened his clenched fist and showed the seamen the few brown grains he had scraped from the inside of the *Samarkand's* hull.

'Look,' he said. 'See how moist they are. These are only flakes of rust to you. Just plain rust, the same rust you detest chipping from the ship's side, and it's quite harmless in itself.

You don't have to fear it ordinarily, especially on deck. But whenever you see it like this again, between decks, and it is as moist as this, look out. Get to the open air fast. Otherwise you'll die.'

The sailors watched in silence as 'The Cat' left their ship to return to his laboratory. His tests on the rust particles revealed the traces of chloride that proved the ballast water had once been salt or brackish.

Taylor also examined two ounces of blood from each of the bodies as soon as they had been raised from the hold.

'I examined these specimens for the presence of carbon monoxide, cyanogen, and hydrogen sulphide,' he recorded later that night. 'The tests were quite negative – that is, there were no poisonous gases whatever in the blood.'

Nor had he expected to find them, because the key to the riddle of the *Samarkand* was already clear in his mind.

'The debris I tested consisted of one ounce of wet oxide of iron resembling in consistency wet putty,' he wrote in his report. 'Mainly it was typical red ferric oxide with dark, almost black, small cores of oxide of iron which crushed under a spatula and gave a core of white fluid (less than one drop) which was faintly alkaline to litmus, being probably unstable ferric hydroxide. The dark material and fluid, when dried in the atmosphere, turned to typical rust. This material dissolved completely in hydrochloric acid. It contained faint traces of sulphide and also a little carbonate. This is a characteristic progressive formation of rust on the surface of iron and steel in wet, enclosed space in which air exists.

'No one would have died had the *Samarkand* gone under cargo from Holland to Bone, or if the ship's ballast tanks had merely been filled with fresh river water. But salt was in the water she took aboard in Holland, and when these ballast tanks were pumped out at Bone, as the phosphate cargo was being loaded, two things happened. The salt air in the ballast tanks was quickly moistened by the heat of the steam in those fuel pipes which I had seen passing through the ballast tanks to the furnaces. Some of the salt in the ballast water had previously caked on the inside of the hull and the bulkheads, and this, too, was moistened by the moist salt air. This moist and cooked salt helped the steel to oxidise, or rust, at quite a fast rate. As this rust was forming, it acted like a vacuum cleaner. It sucked all the oxygen from the air in the closed tanks, and left a much higher-than-normal percentage of nitrogen. Man's senses are unable to detect nitrogen.

'Air contains by volume 21 parts of oxygen and 78 parts of nitrogen per 100, with additional inert gas and carbon monoxide, with variable amounts of water vapour. When oxygen is taken from the air, as in this case, the inert, non-life-sustaining nitrogen is left in more than normal quantities. Maintenance of life becomes more difficult as the percentage of oxygen decreases. When man breathes atmosphere in which oxygen is reduced to 4.2 per cent, he becomes unconscious in six to nine minutes. The inside of the *Samarkand's* tanks gave at least 2,350 square feet on which rust could form.

'If ferric oxide, or rust, were spread on the surface of the tank at the rate of just *one* ounce to twelve square feet, it would be quite sufficient to have absorbed *all* the oxygen in that air. But the rust I found was in the proportion of thirty ounces to twelve square feet!

'These tanks had been sealed for eighty days, and the abstraction of the oxygen was harsh and complete, leaving inert nitrogen in those high quantities. However, the men did not actually die from inhaling this nitrogen. They were killed by anoxia, absolute oxygen starvation.

'It was fortunate that a seaman took the lead and proceeded ahead of me when we went below. He walked steadily and deliberately. None of his actions or movements were out of the ordinary. It was only when that seaman described his stumbling that the truth became obvious. He mentioned pitching head over heels. But he did not do this. He imagined it. Fortunately I was walking behind him and knew that his every step was normal.

'Actually, he had felt the first typical effects – a heightened imagination – of the oxygen lack that quickly overpowered and killed four strong men and nearly trapped others.'

11 | The Dissenter

MYSTERY multiplied for Taylor on all sides when Australia got the jitters in the third year of the Second World War. Crime and disaster kept the mild-mannered man at full alert for weeks or months on end. But more and more – and especially when invasion threatened and the whole of the nation's gold reserve was secretly transported inland and stacked in the cells of Broken Hill's old gaol while a last-ditch stand was planned – he was drawn into other different kinds of problems by anxious officials eager for him to find a solution for them.

Two examples from his casebook are typical of the challenges he accepted on their behalf.

* * *

None of the drivers who flogged the fleets of huge petrol tankers along the Sydney-Melbourne Princes Highway more than twenty years ago is aware that more than one were nearly pounced on as Japanese or Nazi saboteurs and spies. Under the sweeping National Security Regulations the bracket of charges embraced conspiracy, threatening the total war effort, theft and sabotage.

Australia went to war in September, 1939, soon after Britain had declared war on Germany. But it was not until after February, 1942, when bombs had rained on Darwin and Japanese midget submarines were in Sydney Harbour, that many Australians realised how fast the war had spread southward. Australia, to become the bastion of the South Pacific after the oceanic blitzkrieg swamped most territory in the north, was told bluntly to expect shortages and sacrifices if the enemy was to be held back while forces were marshalled to turn the tide.

The days of plenty vanished overnight. Tea, butter and sugar became almost as prized as gold. Suits were rationed, shirt-tails shortened, rubber controlled, beer restricted, racing curtailed. Houses and streets were darkened at night and thousands of cars were laid up for the duration or fitted with ghastly charcoal burners when strict fuel rationing began.

Tankers that could scrape through were strained to capacity to meet the demands of the emergency and fighting services, and the few fuel ration tickets issued every month to approved civilians became one of the most valuable black market commodities.

There are men still living on fortunes made in a few months as they turned out counterfeit tickets in thousands in a now-defunct Australian newspaper office and sold them at outrageous prices.

Typical of them was a Sydney man who revealed to me how he had hauled in £100,000 from black market petrol in one year, after he had abandoned his last shreds of patriotism. That was the year the army, disregarding all protests and proof that he had been invalided from the forces after being gassed in the First World War, had flung him into camp and kept him there asthmatically until finally it realised its 'regrettable mistake.'

While he was still fuming, the tankers rumbled up the Hume Highway to the mushrooming, ever-spreading camps at Seymour, Puckapunyal and Bonegilla, up the Midlands, Calder and Western Highways to feed the new air-training and fighter bases, down the Gippsland highways to fuel the aircraft at the coastal defence stations, the vehicles of the armoured units, and to supply the Commandos training fast in the hush-hush mountain-locked camps at the tip of Wilson's Promontory.

These were vital studs in the armour-plating of Australian defence, because the enemy had been active in the busy sea-lane from Adelaide, through Bass Strait, to Sydney. We who trained in the Australian and New Zealand Commandos' no-man's-land of 'The Prom' in 1941-2 can remember the many nights when staccato messages 'from someone at highest echelon' sent us fanning along the wild south coast, watching through the night for flares or other signs of Japanese or German submarines, or flat-tops reported to be on preliminary reconnaissance or waiting for our ships as they 'turned the bend' at Gabo lighthouse.

There are some who remember the secret anxiety at Dandenong, the gateway from Melbourne to the Gippsland district, when the 6th Australian Brigade was stationed there and its intelligence personnel hunted an Italian demolition group which somehow had escaped internment and planned to gelignite every culvert down the highways.

Tension was high along this belt in 1943. It was boosted suddenly by many deficiencies in bulk fuel supply. Taylor was called in on so many cases that they became routine and almost followed a set pattern. Among them were colossal thefts of fuel for personal gain, but these came to a halt when Taylor conceived the plan of secreting a colourless powder in the tanks of the biggest suspect transports.

That treated petrol trapped the thieves and their receivers because it turned a bright and betraying pink immediately suspects were detained and a soapy solution was dropped in the fluid by police or Commonwealth officers.

Spy fever soared when water was found in millions of gallons of petrol sent to tactical stations along the south and south-east coasts. Paralysis of coastal defence and the dislocation of RAAF training and seaward operations were considered possible when defence chiefs called in Taylor on the case.

He was informed that the police had narrowed their suspicions to one transporting unit and found traces of a foreign liquid in one big tanker.

Taylor analysed a fuel specimen from the tanker and corroborated their suspicions. The foreign agent in the fuel was water, he agreed, but was not convinced saboteurs had been at work.

He insisted that this new case had significant differences from those he had already investigated. If this was sabotage, it was a clumsy and heavy-handed effort, he went on. Would enemy agents make repeated journeys with a fuel that would quickly make its deficiencies evident? If the war effort was to be disrupted at this stage, wouldn't it be more reasonable that the nation's widespread fuel supply should be contaminated in one efficient move?

On the other hand, if this turned out to be an attempt at theft for gain, like others, would any thief be so foolish as to adulterate fuel with water deliberately and hope to escape detection?

With sabotage or theft ruled out, there was only one alternative – accident. There was only one way to decide the issue, he believed, and that provided quite a job. He prepared to call for samples of every type of water that could be found along the relevant defence belt.

Further samples were drawn from the quarantined tanker, and others from every water-supply point a driver could have used sixty-four miles down the Princes Highway through Dandenong, Pakenham and Drouin to the Warragul district. When every specimen had been analysed by him, 'The Cat' was again able to act as much in the interests of innocent drivers as in the interests of harried security officers.

He drew on his incomparable knowledge of his homeland to prove that the components of fresh water varied in many districts of every State. He demonstrated that the water of Warragul, like that of Melbourne's Yarra River and every point between these two limits, contained only one and a half parts of sodium chloride, common salt, in a hundred thousand parts of the water. The type of water along this belt, he said, happened to be so different from many other waters outside these limits that there was practically no chemical relationship.

Now, if petrol had been contaminated along this Melbourne-Warragul belt, which the drivers had to take, that was the salt content the contaminated tankers should have held. But, he postulated, the water he had isolated from the petrol specimens given him from a suspect tanker had contained no less than three per cent of this sodium chloride – that is, a concentration of no less than three parts in a hundred.

In short, its concentration of salt was two thousand times

greater than that of the fresh water of Melbourne and the country districts at least as far as Warragul. Out, therefore, went the theory that contamination could have happened between Melbourne and Warragul, and in came Taylor's remarkable deduction by remote control.

Three per cent corresponded to the salt content of the sea-water along the coast, he pointed out, and at the Melbourne port where the overseas tanker fleets had discharged their cargoes and the road tankers had been filled. Why not check at all Port Melbourne piers and oil wharves? he suggested. He had satisfied himself that there had been no sabotage or theft.

The check was made, and an important leak was discovered – in a bulk petrol-supply line from a tanker berth that had accidentally fouled with salt-water pipes along the wharves!

* * *

It had been a wet and miserable October around the south-eastern corner of the Australian continent, foreshadowing a scorching summer that would crack the earth and wither growth stimulated by the first true burst of spring for weeks.

The Second World War was over the horizon, but some who were sampling new-found comforts after an acute depression had an almost studied disregard for the drum-beating up north. Business was beginning to boom again, trade pacts had been sealed, exports were zooming, and new buildings were changing the skylines of Australian State capitals.

It was in this uneasy last summer of peace that Taylor was saddled with the riddle of the horses and the King's men.

At Tooradin, a sleepy fishing hamlet on Westernport Bay, great scoops had been tearing out building sand for the projects of the Plowright Albion Kooweerup Washed Sand and Gravel Company. This firm had about ten young and healthy work horses, and there was no good reason why any should be taken sick or die.

There were no misgivings when one of the horses died, or when a second died next day. But within a week nine were dead and the one sick survivor refused to eat or drink and stood dejectedly at a paddock gate.

The sand-scooping programme was suspended while a team of police, scientists and company officials searched for evidence of wilful killing or possible epidemic. Veterinary surgeons and the Government pathologist ruled out the possibility of epidemic and left the next move to the Government Analyst. No one was willing to give a ruling here, not even the cagey 'Cat.'

He agreed that it was possible the animals had been deliberately poisoned, for he had examined the contents of the horses' stomachs and found strong traces of arsenic among rock salt, chaff and grass. There was no doubt that the main source of the poison was in a pool, a natural depression in the grazing paddock, which had been filled by heavy October rain.

This finding was enough to convince some people that the company was the victim of a saboteur. But opinion was divided. Others were equally convinced that sabotage was an illusion in a country like Australia and that the work team had been marked down for wanton slaughter by a crank. But on one point all agreed. Whatever the motive, the poisoning was deliberate because the paddock was in a very isolated spot. Very few people passed it, and the poisoned pool was a hundred and fifty yards from trains that passed along the Melbourne-Gippsland tracks.

Taylor dissented with this majority opinion. Had he not been a calculating analyst with a reputation built on patience and a sharp eye for detail, he may easily have agreed with the sabotage theory. Almost certainly, none could successfully have disputed the verdict offered by the Government man. With equal certainty, there were few sufficiently skilled to make him revise his opinion. For not once had Charles Anthony Taylor been proved wrong.

So, as matters stood with many, the pool could have been drained, the horses replaced, and a sharp police watch kept as work went on. But Taylor would have none of it.

A glint in the eyes of the single surviving horse was one of the first factors that held him back from agreeing with the others.

'It's not in line with the attitude expected of a scientist to take hints from a sick horse,' Taylor told me later. 'But the utter dejection of that animal intrigued me. He had a wary glint in his eye and refused to drink pool water anywhere in the district. Nothing I could do would change his mind. He drank only when I led him far away and encouraged him with a bucket filled at a distant house. I wondered if he had an animal instinct about something in the district, and I concluded that he was alive mainly because he happened to be the youngest, strongest and most resistant to disease of the original team.

'His aversion to the big pool and its surroundings was so marked I had the impression that, even if I drained the pool, he'd still refuse to drink. I decided to have another good look round the neighbourhood.'

A suspicion was shaping in the analyst's mind. It was not strong enough to persuade him to voice even a guarded opinion, but it was sufficiently substantial for him to warn the company that no horses or other animals should use the paddock, whether or not the general pool were drained. His intuition and long experience were advising him that, although this was an isolated incident, it was one that could easily be repeated and develop into a vicious cycle – one that might also become a menace to humans.

Provided with a field sketch, Taylor went back to his laboratory to study his notes. He had observed that the area was fairly flat and sandy, but there was a slight rise from the pool towards the railway tracks. Midway between the pool and those tracks was a surfaced road about sixty feet wide, and running parallel with the tracks. There were few houses in the district, and only one or two in view.

Taylor telephoned the Weather Bureau and obtained the local weather reports of the preceding month. There had been long and steady falls of rain in the area before the horses died. Yet most pools had dried out, and even the twelve-inch-deep stormwater trenches along the railway tracks were dry.

He made another phone call. This time a Victorian Government Railways official provided him with the movements of every ganger who had been in the Tooradin district over the past few weeks. But the official was puzzled by the next request made by the analyst.

'You ask us to dig postholes?' he queried over the phone.

'You seriously suggest I send gangers just to dig a few holes and see if water seeps up? Can't the horses be taken somewhere else to drink?'

But Taylor as usual got his way. The postholes were dug.

Afterwards the railway official rang up the analyst. 'Look here, Mr Taylor,' he said. 'My men have dug fresh holes in that paddock, and they have water seeping into them. It seems that this water is polluted, too.'

'I'm not surprised,' said 'The Cat.' 'Didn't you tell me earlier that one of your gangs had been using four-hundred-gallon tanks of arsenic, and that recently they had used it after the heavy rains to kill off spring weeds along the railway line, so that they would not dry and increase the summer fire risk?'

'That's correct,' the officer said. 'But you can't seriously suggest this arsenic was used to kill those horses and endanger people's lives?'

'In a sense, yes,' Taylor answered, and went on to explain to a very worried official: 'I'm only trying to point out that, as I see it (and he was right) the owners will claim damages from the Victorian Railways. Yet there is a simple but surprising explanation to all this.

'When your gangers were spraying those tracks several weeks ago, they doubtless realised the danger of the arsenic they were using, and, bowyang style, wrapped their boots and trouser turn-ups with strips of protective hessian. These rags prevented the spray from damaging their boots and clothes.

'Now at this time the stormwater trenches parallel to the tracks were full of rainwater. That water has since been dried up by the heat. But I'm afraid quite a lot of arsenic got into those ditches at the time. I could see as much when I was prowling around the area the other day. Something obviously was wrong, I thought at the time, because there wasn't a single blade of grass growing along the trenches where the water had been deepest.'

'But,' the railway official countered, 'even if arsenic did get into those trenches, the horses did not drink from them. They were fenced off from their paddocks, and you said they drank from the pool inside the paddock, one that's a hundred and fifty yards from our line.'

'Quite so,' 'The Cat' agreed. 'But hear me out. When your trenches were full the poisoned water from them actually seeped a hundred and fifty yards down the slope to that pool, which is a natural depression. It did not trickle down the surface. It first seeped down to the sub-strata of soil and sand, and then went trickling methodically downhill and right under the road until it settled in that big pool and in smaller ones farther down. This is not a case of sabotage or wanton killing of livestock. It was just an unfortunate oversight by those who forget that arsenic is durable. It cannot be destroyed. But it is slightly soluble in water, and it will flow with that water to wherever the water flows.'

The railway official was silent before saying: 'So some of our men must be held responsible, Mr Taylor? They poured arsenic in those trenches. But were they grossly negligent, wilful, or just damned careless? Tell me that.'

'On the contrary,' said 'The Cat.' 'I assure you they were very careful men. They wore bowyang cuffs to protect their feet. Well, as they had expected, by the end of the day's work these rags had become soaked with the arsenic solution. How were they to know what mischief could result from rinsing the hessian strips in those full stormwater ditches? Remarkable, isn't it, how death can lurk behind a most innocent and well-intentioned act?'

12 Guilt - in Black and White

MANY policemen of the old school groaned when 'The Wee Alick Duncan' arrived in Australia in 1937 to become Chief Commissioner of the Victoria Police. His brusqueness angered some of them and his imperious outlook ruffled others. True, the white-haired Highland Scot with the machine-gun voice and the bunched-up shoulders of a bison gave little promise that he intended to endear himself or care a hoot about being the controversial figure of his force.

Alexander Mitchell Duncan, aided by a Government eager for changes after a top-level scandal in the force, made sweeping operational reforms that were years overdue. He brought the fingerprint expert, Alec Martin, back from the banishment imposed by the former Commissioner only because Martin justifiably had claimed a few shillings specialist's allowance that would be automatic now. He persuaded Australia to join Interpol, and put the country on police maps from Europe to the Far East. He encouraged the founding and development of a scientific bureau, and because he had worked with men like Sir Bernard Spilsbury he recognised that his force should have even a closer alliance with the shrewd Government Analyst, 'The Cat.'

As Duncan reached his objective – namely, to be able to have every bit of available talent assembled at a crime scene without delay – Taylor came more into public focus and his name became more familiar in the press. Before long it was featured in the great crime stories of the day, as when George Green, a chimney sweep, was about to die for double murder and bold type proclaimed: 'One of the most grimly fascinating features was the evidence given by the Government Analyst, Mr Charles Anthony Taylor.'

I recall that evidence whenever my eyes rest on a fading document pinned to my study feature wall. It is the original copy of Green's appeal to the Full Court after he had been convicted and had asked to be present at the appeal on the grounds that his conviction was against the evidence, that it was wrongly and improperly admitted, and that the jury had been misdirected by the learned judge, Mr Justice (Sir Charles) Lowe, of whom Australia's Prime Minister, Sir Robert Menzies, said: 'I would like to be as wise as Sir Charles Lowe looks.'

Sir Charles Lowe not only appeared wise. He was as wise as he appeared, and thorough and fair to boot. He had taken the trial of Green with his usual resolution that everything relative to the case on either side would be produced and rigorously examined in his court. Even the scrupulously prepared evidence of the Government Analyst he would not accept solely on the submitted effort, but only after careful and searching questions of his own.

Chief among the questions Mr Justice Lowe asked as Green's trial was drawing to its close related to the characteristics of human hair. There was an imposing mass of other evidence before him, but the judge – himself growing grey – became very interested in the shades of human hair the scientist was submitting to the court.

'You have told us,' he said to Taylor, 'that these fine strands of hair you have laid before us are white in colour, and that they could have belonged only to the white-haired head of the elderly woman who was killed.'

That was so, the analyst assured him firmly. All hair had pigment except white. And white hair, which came only with age, came about when the pigment faded. Greyness was an illusion, the analyst continued. He had established as much during the trial of Colin Ross, after the murder of Alma Tirtschke in Gun Alley when he had proved that greyness was a combination of coloured hairs *and* white.

The accused man, Green, must have felt a new shaft of hope burn through him as the judge leaned down to direct another searching question to the analyst.

'White hairs come with age, Mr Taylor? But let me put this question to you. What do we say about white-headed children, the "Snowies" and "Chalkies" of our boyhood days?'

The inference was clear enough. Could it, for example, be argued that the hairs submitted in this murder evidence as being white had come from the head of a snowy child?

Taylor shook his own greying head.

'Not a chance, Your Honour,' he said. 'The hairs of a snowy child are never white. They, too, are pigmented. For they are cream.'

It was the last earthly lesson that George Green learned.

He had also learned, too late, that if only he had taken the trouble to wash his hands and brush or shake his clothes, he may not have been sentenced to hang for the brutal murders of a spinster and her teenage niece.

Like many other criminals who have more brawn than brains, however, he made the fatal error of overlooking the tiny things that so often mean more to a judge and jury than even a signed confession.

* * *

George Green the chimney sweep had been drinking high-percentage Australian beer heavily on the afternoon of Saturday, November 12, 1938, and his slow brain buzzed with bold but fuddled notions when he left the suburban pub at 6 p.m., closing time. That was only an hour or two before Mrs Annie Wiseman, who was sixty-five, went to bed in her modest brick villa at Glenroy, an outer Melbourne suburb. She had just said her customary good night to her seventeen-year-old niece, Phyllis, and promised to awaken her in time for Sunday morning service.

By morning both were dead. They had been strangled with bare hands, lighting flex, and clothing. There were signs in the house of fierce struggles, and of an intruder who had searched wildly for loot. The bodies, in disarranged night clothes, were found on the floor by a Mrs Rowland Barrett when, by a previous arrangement, she called at the house to take the aunt and her niece to church.

Before noon that Sunday a detective telephoned Taylor at his Gardenvale home and asked him to examine the bodies when they reached the city morgue. If possible, the analyst was then to join the detectives on the spot, for the case already promised to be one of those where deadly trifles were to be sought rather than conventional clues.

Taylor left the corpses in the morgue and, as he drove on to Glenroy, mulled over one small detail. It was the colour of Mrs Annie Wiseman's hair. In his judgment it was dead white, without a shade of pigment left in it. He could not avoid remembering how, fifteen years earlier, he had helped to hang Colin Ross by his evidence relating to human hairs. Crime history might well repeat itself, he thought.

Detective-Inspector Harry (the Wolf) Carey, Detective-Sergeant Fred Sickerdick, Senior Detective Fred Delminico, and Detective Frank Delaney were among the detectives who had searched the Wiseman villa by the time 'The Cat' arrived there. They were glad to see him, for they were intrigued and puzzled by the torn-off corner of an old milk delivery bill they had found on the floor with several copper and silver coins and dead matches scattered on the carpet between the places where the bodies had been found. But there had been no time to search for links to prove if it were a fragment of a household account, or whether it could have been dragged from the pocket of an intruder when he was, for instance, fumbling for a box of matches.

The dust on one window ledge had been disturbed, but the theory that the killer had escaped that way was dismissed. For one thing, both front and back doors had been found open. For another, there were no revealing footprints on the garden bed below the ledge. It appeared more likely that the murderer had intended to leave that way, but perhaps had deliberately disturbed the dust to leave a misleading trail.

If this were so he had made a serious error, because the police and 'The Cat' were soon convinced, by the nature of the injuries inflicted, that the attacker must have been quite a strong man who could hardly have avoided leaving an imprint on that garden bed. It was therefore likely that the killer had left his print on the open doors.

But here the searchers faced temporary defeat. After most of the house had been dusted with fine French chalk, not one print for which the detectives could not account was found.

The detectives were discussing this negative result when Taylor grubbed out of the carpet a few tiny grains of black powder which smudged easily when rubbed.

Back in his laboratory he established that the grains were those of household soot. The crime team received their second break when the torn scrap of milk bill went on Taylor's microscope platform.

There was a dark smudge or smear across one corner of that scrap, and Taylor satisfied himself that this was made by household chimney soot. The other investigators agreed with him that neither of the gentle and fastidious Wisemans had left these traces on the bill or carpet. So it was likely that the killer had brought the piece of milk bill to the house.

Could the suspect be a chimney sweep? One with a powerful grip. A halfpenny proved that. It was stuck to Mrs Wiseman's wrist. Both of her wrists had been pressed savagely on to the carpet during her battle for survival, and the coin lying on the carpet had become so firmly embedded in the flesh that it had to be prised out with a knife blade.

While Senior-Constable Haygarth and an aboriginal black-tracker were following the faint track of a bicycle leading away from the house, Delminico and others were 'legging' the sprawling district and seeking the possible owner of the milk bill scrap. Their check on all dairies that might have circulated such bills took them to hundreds of customers in seven suburbs inside an area nearly eight miles long and two miles wide. The three chief suburbs were Glenroy, Coburg and Thornbury, almost in a straight line, but five and a half, and two miles, apart respectively.

The detectives' patience and tenacity were rewarded. They found a woman who recognised the fragment because it was her handwriting on the piece. She said that on November 3, nine days before the murders, she had left her house at Thornbury and moved to Coburg, closer to Glenroy.

Four days later, on November 7, a man had called at her new house at Coburg and asked if she wanted a job done on the spot. She told the man she was not interested at the moment as she had just moved from Thornbury. The man then asked if those who had taken her Thornbury house might want him to do a job. She told him they might because the chimneys had not been swept in the two or three years before she left the Thornbury house. To help him, she had written her old address on a milk bill, torn off the receipted part to keep, and given the other piece to the man.

He was a chimney sweep, about forty years old, the woman told the police, and the address she had written for him *was* the one detectives were now showing her on the paper scrap.

It was not long afterwards that the police called at a house at Heidelberg to interview a chimney sweep named George Green, who hotly denied the crimes. He agreed he had been given the scrap of milk bill by the woman the police had found at Coburg. But he insisted he had been unable to do the job and had given the scrap of paper to two wandering knockabout sweeps in search of work. He threw out other cunning alibis and would not be shaken from assurances that he could explain and prove his innocent movements throughout the murder day and night.

However, the police were sure they had their man. But without fingerprints or other evidence, how would they prove conclusively that Green actually had been inside the Wisemans' house?

'The Cat' had the answer up his dustcoat sleeve.

He reasoned that the killer must be a powerful man. The Government pathologist, Dr Crawford Mollison, had told him there was severe bruising on the back of Mrs Wiseman's head, and shown that her head had been savagely jerked from side to side before she died. She had been found on the floor, and her head had been bumped heavily on that carpeted floor while she struggled desperately for her life.

Taylor returned to the Wiseman villa. He and Delminico found that the heavy pile of the carpet where Mrs Wiseman's head had lain was slightly flatter and a little more tangled than the surrounding parts.

Deep in the disturbed pile Taylor came across a few short pieces of hair. Dead-white hair. This dismissed the slightest lingering doubt that the elder woman could have strangled her niece and then killed herself. This was definitely a case of double murder with evidence that Mrs Wiseman had been battered down when rising to investigate a commotion in her niece's room.

Now there were only two last official steps to take. Taylor examined Mrs Wiseman's dressing-gown again, and from a lapel removed a couple of dislodged, dead-white hairs. He was acting on the assumption that whoever killed Mrs Annie Wiseman would also have been subjected to the general shaking, wrenching and other convulsive body movements, and at one time would have been kneeling over her on the floor.

So he took Green's coat which was frayed and the lining of which was worn with the horsehair stuffing protruding. The strong, sharp hairs had picked up and retained some foreign material. One strand was found inside the worn lapel. Another was plucked from the right side pocket of the coat, and another from Green's trouser turn-up. They were not horsehairs. They were fine human hairs that tapered to a point, and they were dead white.

In length, shade, texture and other pertinent characteristics, each was identical with those found in the carpet pile and on the dressing-gown, and with the specimens Taylor had taken from the elderly woman's white head of hair.

As mentioned earlier, Green appealed to the Full Court against his death sentence, decrying the evidence which the jury had accepted without division. But he was hanged at Pentridge Gaol, five miles from where the women died, on April 17, 1939.

What was the motive for the callous murders? Green would not divulge it because repeatedly he protested he was innocent. But apparently his only gain was the £1 note missing from Annie Wiseman's house, the note she intended to put in the church collection plate the morning after she died, or give, as was her kindly habit, to some beggar or man in search of work who cared to call on her for help.

13 A Real Honey

'I HOPE you're not too sore with me,' the little man said as he sat very upright in Taylor's laboratory in November, 1945. 'I've come a hundred miles from Bendigo to see you because I'm told you're about the only cove who could help me. But maybe you only handle the spectacular cases?'

Taylor encouraged his visitor with a smile. 'I'm listening,' he said.

His visitor fumbled in a pocket and produced a two-ounce jar. 'Well, there you are,' he said, pushing the jar across the table with the gesture of one who is glad suspense is over. 'They're only bees. Dead honey bees. I've got scores of hives at Bendigo. But I've lost bees by the thousand. They're thick on the ground and dying so fast that I'll soon be ruined. And I'm wondering if this epidemic will kill off millions of other bees all over the place and set the crops back hard.'

Taylor gave him a nod. 'What I was thinking, too,' the analyst agreed.

'Unless, of course, someone is getting at me and working off a grudge,' the little man went on.

'Always possible,' Taylor answered. 'But unlikely, I should think. Now, I have to go to Bendigo on a police inquiry. I'll be up to see you Thursday. A lot of things have come my way, but never bees until now.'

The apiarist appeared even more dejected when Taylor kept the date.

'I just don't get it,' he lamented. 'Many of the bees are working as usual. Doesn't seem much wrong with them. Yet I've lost hundreds of others since I saw you.'

Taylor was mooching among the rows of hives. His eyes roved over the carpet of dead bees on the ground. He watched the flights taking off – swarms of nimble, humming, healthy-looking bees peeling off from formations in their endless quest for honey.

'A nice breeze,' he told the apiarist again. 'Not too much, but just enough.'

The man eyed him warily.

'It's a steady current, don't you think?' Taylor said conversationally.

'You mean the wind? I guess so. Frankly, I never thought much about the breeze. More interested in my bees. Breezes don't worry them much.'

Taylor meandered thoughtfully away, the apiarist, silent and moody, following at his heels. He had almost resigned himself to bankruptcy, with an unsolved mystery he could curse for years, when Taylor stopped in the shade of a giant red gum tree and peered across a gully.

'Now take this wind,' the scientist went on. 'So you often have a breeze from that direction. Well, who are those men near that ridge a couple of hundred yards away? Close to that white smoke.'

'Never seen them close to,' the beeman said. 'Just a couple of codgers who came up here about a month ago. They don't belong to the district. Don't know them or what they're doing there.'

'I think you ought to have a word with them,' Taylor told him. 'After all, they're murdering your bees.'

The beeman grinned raggedly.

'Ah, break it down,' he scoffed. 'Those chaps are digging, you can see for yourself. They haven't set foot here. My bees are dropping dead on the ground, and in their hives. How can there be the faintest possible connection?'

Unruffled, Taylor trudged across the gully to the ridge and back again. He looked up into the branches of the giant red gum tree, wet his finger, and held it in the air.

'Soon you'll have nothing to worry about,' he promised calmly.

The man's attitude of scorn and faint hostility turned to one of wonder and gratitude as 'The Cat' continued with an explanation:

'Have you ever noticed that many of your bees fly from their hives to this giant red gum tree? This tree is in the glory of full flower. It's a superb specimen. But probably you didn't know that a red gum tree has a most delectable nectar inside all those prolific flowers.

'Australian honey has a different tang from that of England or, say, Greece. Ours is milder. Our bees do not, as most people seem to think, collect their honey from suburban gardens. True, they take it from the honeysuckle, the giant sunflower, and to a lesser extent the lavender. But the gums are their main source of supply – the yellow box down Gippsland way, and the red tree in this direction.

'You will note, however, that there are many dead bees beneath this lovely tree, yet few under other trees. One reason is that those other trees are not yet in full flower. Another is that they are not in the way of that wind blowing from the direction of those two men with the fire. Most of the smoke they are making is billowing towards this giant tree. Note, also, that the smoke is dense and white.'

The apiarist – not fully convinced, but certainly impressed – interrupted. 'You should know that may drive bees out of trees or hives, but not kill them,' he reminded Taylor.

'Yes, indeed!' Taylor nodded. 'That's why I asked you earlier about the wind. No harm is done on nice days like this. The harm is done when the wind blows more strongly from that direction, strong enough to carry that white smoke straight across to here.'

The little apiarist shook his head. 'I'm with you so far,' he said. 'But I don't remember the bees only dropping dead when strong winds blow and that smoke drifts over here.'

'Exactly,' replied 'The Cat.' 'Several times, however, the smoke has been thick enough to drive them from this tree. But when the wind dropped they swarmed back to the tree again – and died.'

'Why?' asked the puzzled bee-keeper.

Taylor pointed his cigarette across the gully. 'Those men are "cooking",' he explained. 'They are roasting "fool's gold." We know it as pyrites. They're trying to get the sulphur out of it for commercial use.'

'So that's it!' The beeman sounded angry. 'The sulphur has been killing off my bees!'

'No,' Taylor continued patiently, 'that's not it. Far from it. The sulphur remains at the furnace. It isn't in the smoke at all.'

'Then . . .' But words failed a very confused apiarist.

Taylor gave him a look intended to be encouraging. 'It's a pity that brick chimney those men have built isn't a few feet higher,' he remarked. 'It may then have helped the wind to disperse that smoke. However, I'm sure that's something you can help them fix. But you'd better do it soon,' he warned, 'because there is death in the pyrites those fellows are roasting. The roasting process has been releasing a deadly poison from the pyrites – arsenic, which has risen from that chimney as a fine white powder. Hence white smoke. This is what happened,' he went on. 'On days when the wind is strongest in this direction these fine but deadly particles of arsenic have been sticking to the delicious nectar on the stamens of those red gum blossoms. It was like a drop of poison in a goblet of Borgia wine.'

Indeed a rare combination, Taylor reflected, as the train took him home. A very old, repaired pyrites kiln not far from a new bee farm. A chimney stack that would have been high enough on the goldfields of the past, but was too low for modern times. A variable breeze and, right in its way, the one giant tree with thousands of blossoms yielding the very nectar bees craved.

In all, a remarkable combination – a real honey!

14 The Riddle of the RAAF

I COULD always understand why Charles Anthony Taylor was not once discredited in Australian courts when I waited for him carefully to choose his words and saw his eyes narrow to slits behind his steel-rimmed spectacles. Furthermore, it never surprised me at times when he grew confidential with me to hear him decide that his outstanding case – at least the one that gave him the fullest measure of personal satisfaction – was not a murder, as one may have expected.

It was, he confided, the riddle of the Royal Australian Air Force, one of Australia's biggest secrets of the Second World War. His part in it gratified him because the lives of so many Australian airmen were saved after many of the RAAF's heroes had been lost.

Several years ago Taylor and I were the first to make an open challenge that the RAAF had concealed an unpleasant secret ever since the great surrender. Our records leave no doubt of that. We alleged that scores of airmen had died mysteriously during war-time training at a country base and that the public had never been told. The RAAF remained aloof and silent at the time. Yet, oddly or significantly, it did not challenge Taylor's records through the years that followed, and it remained silent until 1961 when, quite unexpectedly, corroborative evidence came from an officer who should be qualified to know. Only then, with the secret of so many crashes twice uncovered, did the RAAF break the silence of almost twenty years and advance a theory which Taylor and this officer repudiate in full and are never likely to accept.

Both refuse to alter their conviction that Australians died accidentally but tragically from deadly poison gas. The RAAF now belatedly maintains – although it has declined to publish its secret inquiry's findings – that every one of the airmen died through a small but vital mechanical defect in his machine.

This makes the story even more intriguing, and at least the controversy it produced revealed one issue that had not seen the light before – namely, over some eighteen months of Australia's war crisis, the casualties from only two RAAF stations in the Gippsland district were about 100 machines destroyed completely, lost at sea without a trace or damaged beyond repair on land, and about 150 aircrew dead.

All without a shot being fired.

Small wonder that anything known, suspected, or to be suggested should be told, even at this late date.

I shall reveal all available reliable facts about this disaster because the years may have softened the memories for relatives of those who died under what must have been terrifying circumstances even to the most sacrificially brave, and also because this is an essential chapter of trial, endeavour and – who knows? – error in a country producing men who will make it great.

I consulted many before I led up to this story with the facts I have gathered in the past years. They included police, scientists, RAAF members from sergeant to Air rank, and a Crown pathologist. Among the number is one who berated me on one occasion for not accepting the RAAF's tardy explanation of the case; but who, a week later, admitted after deep thought: 'If Taylor had a good sample of blood – and now I can see he must have had – then there must be a bloody lot in the finding he brought out. And I say that as a medical scientist and as a former pilot who heard of the RAAF's trim-tab theory.'

Several of those I spoke to have reason to remember how the sad chapter of calamities led to real alarm and acrimonious accusations of 'murder' and 'mass suicide.' At least two recall the trenchant protests of a very senior officer – now a judge –

who, I am assured, was threatened with court-martial for his outspoken comments within the Service. That is why I wonder, when at least unanimity on the magnitude of the tragedy has been reached, why every report that was made cannot even now be brought forward for the public here and in Britain to read. Until this happens we will never know how many British planes, or how many Australian models, contributed to this dreadful toll of lives and material, whether the tragedies were caused by faulty British manifolds, or whether there were faulty tail-trim tabs that have to share the blame.

Two men vitally concerned in the official investigation insist that manifolds were to blame.

One is the man who was never proved wrong, Charles Anthony Taylor.

First, his story.

* * *

It has its beginning in 1917, although no one had reason to know it then, at the meal table of a typical country family in the middle of Victoria about the time the first of the American forces were landing in France to strengthen the Western Front. Then there was a long span of silence – no link until almost a quarter of a century later, when British and Australian aircraft factories were turning out machines at an unprecedented rate to join American air fleets plotting a course to Tokyo.

The story concerns two small cities, both in the Victorian countryside, during two world wars. It could not have been written, and the riddle of the RAAF may never have been solved, if Taylor had not been seeking a home for himself and the coming family; if he had not been of friendly and amiable disposition; if he had not stored such knowledge that those who met him could forget him; and if he had not decided what he wanted to be until relatively late in his youth.

Most determined and energetic men are confidently and comfortably hoeing the furrows of their careers before they are thirty-two. But Taylor, at this age in 1917, had about three more years to live before he realised that his only mission in life could be that of a dedicated medico-legal chemist. He wanted something solid, and he was avoiding callings that may have produced profit without providing achievement. He was looking for the mould into which all his knowledge and power to reason could be poured.

The McPherson family knew this in 1917 at Benalla, on the flats of north-east Victoria where Ned Kelly and his bush-ranging gang had roamed and plundered only forty years earlier. Taylor, a capable science and mathematics master at the local high school, boarded at the McPherson home with his wife and the first of his five children while he was seeking his destiny and waiting, meanwhile, for his first home to be built. The older McPhersons enjoyed their boarder's intense interest in everything around him. Their daughter listened raptly to Taylor's tributes to the quality of the country's orchids and bush flowers, and young Clyde McPherson, only seventeen, had the normal teenager's suspicion of all school-masters, but liked this one. Taylor seemed so simple, human, and understanding of others' problems, Clyde told me more than forty years later, that he never forgot his wisdom and advice.

McPherson, now sixty-five, still remembers that young teacher's determination to conquer any problem within his reach.

'Mr Taylor stayed with us about six months,' he told me. 'In those days we owned magnificent jumping and hunting horses. Mr Taylor, always a pioneer, owned one of the first one-stroke Douglas motor-cycles, quite a novelty of those times. I was as determined to ride that as Charlie was to master horsemanship and ride a hunter. We made a deal to teach each other. He had the laugh on me when, after only two lessons, I went for my first ride. I had forgotten how to stop, and I was afraid to turn the machine until I came to a vast clearing where an aircraft could have landed. I had to cling to that infernal machine until its petrol ran out and it spluttered to a halt.

'Then I gave Charlie his first mount – a hunter with steely eyes and a really hard mouth. Both came out of the stable all right, but then the charger took over. There was an unforget-table gallop through the town with Charlie flat on the horse's back and clinging to mane and leather for dear life. When the canny horse had shaken up every bone in Charlie's body he streaked for home, thundered into the loose box with Charlie still glued to the saddle, and came to a sickening halt. If the rider had been upright in the saddle he would have been decapitated, and Australia would never have had its eminent crime chemist.'

Some twenty-six years passed. Taylor had become a renowned crime chemist and often was styled police analyst because so many of his duties were concerned with police investigations.

On May 5, 1941, the first Bristol Beaufort bomber came off the assembly lines at Fishermen's Bend, a fast-expanding industrial area along the south bank of Melbourne's Yarra River. It was a twin-engined torpedo-carrying and reconnaissance and general purpose aircraft made under licence from the British Government. Those made in Australia were to supplement the many England had shipped and had promised to ship. The Australian models, unlike those made in Britain, had American engines, twin Pratt and Whitney Wasps.

The Beaufort was the first real bomber Australia had built, and it became the first modern one the RAAF had in any quantity. About seven hundred were built before production stopped in August, 1944.

While production was in full blast, hundreds of airmen were being pushed through special training and conversion courses on airfields outside Sale and Bairnsdale, on the Gippsland coastal strip between Sale and Lakes Entrance.

Many were veterans from several war theatres. They included Pathfinders and other decorated aces, and there were a good number who had not been in combat. But all were packing as many flying hours as possible into the machines, British and Australian, that were shortly to be hated and feared as 'the Bogey Beauforts.'

'They became known as a sheer bastard of an aircraft,' one RAAF veteran told me.

Mr Frank Doak, who still has an appointment in the Service, said: 'I was flying in Australia at the time. The long chapter of disasters was kept as hush-hush as possible, but the fact that something was tragically wrong ultimately trickled to every airfield in Australia. Morale dropped so low that most aircrew types would fight like hell to avoid being posted to Beaufort training.'

That seems to describe the atmosphere in 1943 when a minor routine job took Taylor to Bairnsdale, chief town of the county of that name, a hundred and eighty miles east of Melbourne. There are eight hotels and seven banks at Bairnsdale. There would be nothing significant in that at any time other than this particular day when the presence of one of each led to the first invisible clue to a local but stupendous national secret.

Taylor finished his routine inquiry early in the day. The next train to Melbourne was not due for several hours. He knew only few of the Bairnsdale folk, but decided to look up an old friend, the manager of one of the seven banks. They went out for a glass of ale and debated which hotel would suit them best.

'Might be quieter if we went to the small pub across the way,' the manager suggested. 'There are hundreds of RAAF men in the town. Been here for weeks. I've never seen so many different types and ranks. They have taken over every hotel in town except this one.'

It was just small talk made by the bank manager, but Taylor's inquisitive nature could not be changed by a stack of security regulations.

'It does seem like a lot of airmen, particularly brass, for a place like this,' he said as he glanced up and down the street. 'A lot even for an air base area.'

'The real brass have not been here long,' his banker friend went on. 'They came down from the city a few weeks ago, I think, but I wouldn't know for certain. We don't ask questions down here because it isn't the done thing. We wouldn't get any answers, anyway. All the same, something fishy must be going on. You can feel it. Another thing, a butcher was fined twenty pounds down here the other day. Charged under the Security Regulations. He won't say why, and the town doesn't know much about it. But we gather he had talked a bit too freely about a body, or several bodies, or disappearances, or something to that effect. The fact is, anyway, that the authorities went for him and properly silenced him.'

'I wonder why?' said Taylor.

The banker let it go at that, but Taylor was not satisfied.

'I could feel the apprehension in the air,' he explained to me. 'Everywhere I went in the town I could sense foreboding, a kind of heavy unhappy feeling about the place, and yet there was nothing to indicate a reason. Later I decided to pay my usual courtesy call on the local police before I left.'

There are about twenty policemen at Bairnsdale headquarters and district today. There were fewer than a dozen when Taylor went down there, but any one of this number could have been on duty when he walked in.

Taylor found himself looking at a tired face as the first constable in the swivel chair glanced up from a paper-cluttered desk. He had met this man before, he was sure of that, but a long time back. His lips pursed characteristically, he stared at the waiting policeman. Then his eyes narrowed and he smiled as he put out his hand.

'Isn't it Clyde?' he said. 'After all these years. Let me see. It must be twenty-six. Well, bless my soul! Clyde McPherson. So you threw in the Benalla estate business and joined the force!'

When the enthusiasm of reunion had passed Taylor told McPherson he had just dropped in while waiting for a train to take him back from a routine job. He hoped Clyde was having a quiet and relaxed time.

'I'd like to agree,' McPherson replied. 'But I'm sorry to say things have been fairly humming in this town and for miles around. I can tell you, as Crown Analyst, but I dare not open my mouth elsewhere. All of us down here have had a terrific run of wretched inquests.'

He mentioned some names they both knew.

'Charlie Derham at Morwell – remember him? He was the one gravely wounded in the Coles Store hold-up in 1930. Well, he's been flat out at Morwell. Simon Proctor and Victor Vincent have been on the run nearly every day at this station. And like everyone else I've been flat to the board every day.

'The number of aircraft crashes down here has been frightening. Nearly every day. Inquests nearly every day, too. Sometimes two and three bodies a day – often five. Many of them were very good pilots, including instructors. These are the quickest inquests you ever saw. There's no evidence as to why the machines are crashing. The findings are almost automatic ones of misadventure, and if there are any remains the orders for burial are immediate. Most of the planes crashing are Beaufort bombers. There have been a few Hudsons and Oxfords, but they're only a small percentage. It's the Beauforts that really have them worried.

'The strange thing is that most seem to have crashed on land. If any went into the sea, the bodies have not been recovered – nor the planes. When they crash on land, the machines and crews have burned to ashes and left no clues. And no one can tell us why these crashes continue.'

Taylor nodded slowly as he drummed his fingers on the back of a chair.

'Well, Clyde,' he suggested, 'maybe there's an answer somewhere. I would like to be in on this one. Perhaps just one body will be recovered, and then, if I can see samples of the remains, we may find out the reason why these crashes occur.'

Shortly after Taylor returned to Melbourne another Beaufort crashed. He says it plunged into a swamp or lake, without sending out a signal, taking a decorated Pathfinder and his crew with it. All three were drowned. For thirty hours RAAF rescue squads and police dragged and plumbed the bottom until the pilot's body had been recovered. One of those at the scene was Superintendent E. W. Rosewarne, then a squadron-leader and assistant provost-marshal. He remembers the tense effect of the disasters in the district.

'The Air Force was not only concerned,' he told me. 'It was really alarmed. It was a secret the service hoped to guard as tightly as the Spitfire riddle not long before.'

Rosewarne said the RAAF used every appliance within call and worked throughout the night with glaring lights until that body was recovered.

Back in Melbourne Taylor was enjoying one of the rare nights his multiplying duties allowed him at home with a growing family.

'The old telephone on the wall rang about 9 p.m.,' he told me. 'It was an airman speaking from a telephone booth at Flinders Street railway station. He said he had been sent up from Bairnsdale with a glass jar and a small bottle, and what should he do with them? I told him to leave them with an orderly at the city morgue, then at the Batman Avenue side of the Yarra Bank. I would get them from the night orderly's relief first thing in the morning.

'In a two-ounce jar was a piece of human liver. The larger jar was filled with blood. Both specimens had come from the pilot's remains. I was told, on indisputable authority, that they were the first and almost only remains of any of the airmen who had crashed at Bairnsdale.'

Taylor made two tests on each specimen, one with tannic acid and the other with a spectrograph. There was an absorption band in the rainbow of colours refracted by the spectrograph which, in his qualified opinion, would solve the riddle of the RAAF. He sent an initial report to the RAAF on the spot. He said he could explain why no signals had been flashed from the doomed planes, and why every airman who had died was alive, although unable to move or speak, until the very moment of tremendous impact.

Taylor was firm that there had not been sabotage. He insisted that mechanical failures were not to blame. He was positive that the disasters had not been caused by repeated negligence.

'Then the storm broke,' Taylor told me. 'The CO of East Sale aerodrome, Group-Captain W. H. (Bull) Garing, DFC (now Air-Commodore of the RAAF base, Edinburgh, South Australia), disagreed with me. Group-Captain (now Air-Marshal Sir Frederick) Scherger came to see me. It was characteristic of Scherger that he pulled no punches and came straight to the point.

' "Taylor," he said, "I don't think you're right. I feel that this case should have been handled by the RAAF Director of Medical Services, Air-Commodore (the late Sir Victor) Hurley." '

Taylor nodded affably. 'By all means refer it to him,' he said. 'But in the meantime you still feel that the Beaufort is a really good machine, don't you?'

'Yes, I do.'

'It has good fire power?'

'Very good!'

'Most of the pilots flying them are sound?'

'I would say so.'

'In that case, it's a pity they've been poisoned,' Taylor snapped.

'Now what the devil do you mean by that?' demanded Taylor's visitor.

Taylor reached for the specimens.

'I ask you to take these along to Air-Commodore Hurley,' he invited Scherger. 'Let him examine them. But let me tell you now that he can only come to the same conclusion as I. There cannot be the faintest question of the result being otherwise, as you will find.'

The corroborative analysis and report was made for Hurley by Mr Howden at the famed Walter and Eliza Institute, which used a very powerful spectrograph. The report was ready by 4 p.m. that day.

It corresponded exactly with that made earlier by the Government Analyst. But Taylor was too experienced and exact to allow a flush of success to colour his report.

'Deadly carbon monoxide gas has been sweeping back into many of the Beaufort aircraft,' he reported. 'Those who breathed it lost the power to use their arms and legs. Monoxide removed their will-power completely and immediately and made it impossible for them to function normally.

'The pilot, sensing danger, wanted to move his control column, but was almost paralysed. The radio operator knew he should flash a last dramatic and revealing message. But he could not move his hands. All aboard were perfectly aware what they should do, and what they just could not bring themselves to do, and they were well aware of the death coming up to them as they waited for the dreadful moment when they hit the land or the sea.

'These effects were obvious, but had to be proven scientifically, when I saw the colour of the blood in the jar. It was bright cherry red, characteristic of carbon-monoxide effects. The effect was exactly the same as that on British coal miners whose experiences and deaths were investigated thoroughly not long ago by a British Royal Commission.

'The ventilators near the nose in many of these aircraft are not suitable,' he concluded, 'when the aircraft is subject to cross-winds and the engines have been running richly. My finding in these RAAF cases is positive and conclusive.' No more fatal crashes were reported.

Taylor told me that, some time after his report was submitted, he was told that the lessons learned from the catastrophes had been passed to Beaufort manufacturers in Britain and Australia, and that the machines had been modified. In the strange way of coincidence he also had personal evidence that his findings and advice had not been ignored.

'One afternoon I was waiting to collect my winnings in a place tote queue at Flemington racecourse,' he told me. 'A soldier in front of me looked round and spotted an airman friend.

' "Hi, Fred!" he shouted. "How're those blue orchids?"

'The airman came across and said: "Blue orchids be damned. Know what I'm doing now? I'm down at Bairnsdale, and I go up in planes carrying cages of white mice and canaries. Can you beat that for winning a war? There's some crazy old coot who reckons we got poison in our planes." '

'Excuse me,' 'The Cat' broke in. 'Don't you think it just possible that the crazy old coot might be right?'

The airman, suddenly conscious of the security regulations that banned loose talk, gaped at the beaming Taylor, then fled.

So far as Taylor personally was concerned that rounded off the case. Several years passed before any of the mystery became public knowledge, and then only when Taylor was retiring from the Crown service and related the facts for me to publish in outline at the time.

His findings were never denied. Nor was there any official disclosure of the numbers of machines that crashed or of men who died in them.

In some unofficial quarters, however – like the Naval and Military Club of Melbourne – the subject was raised from time to time by veterans like that gallant chevalier, Air-Marshal Adrian (King) Cole whose host of friends ranged from Kingsford-Smith to the Duke of Windsor.

Some had heard of the monoxide findings. But they had left the service with the impression that faulty tail-trim tabs had caused the greatest disaster of the RAAF.

Time and again I returned to Taylor with their theories and reports, but he always remained adamant.

'How and why should I deny that the RAAF did not find aircraft here and there with a tail-trim fault?' he would say each time I told him the fresh opinion. 'But my findings remain unchallenged. No more fatal crashes were reported after my report was sent in.'

But it took until the end of 1961 to prod the RAAF into a confirmation of the Gippsland horrors. That came only after another official, after a gap of several years since Taylor and I first outlined the riddle, referred to disasters shielded too long behind that powerful curtain of National Security Regulations.

This official was Mr Brett-Hilder. He was master of the South Sea Islands trading vessel *Malaita*. In his book, *Navigation in the South Seas*, he revealed that in 1943 the RAAF was losing more aircrew in training than through battle!

British Beaufort aircraft had been built with a heating system to warm the cabins, Mr Brett-Hilder wrote. This was essential for flying conditions over Europe. But because the heater system was not required in the southern hemisphere climate, the hole from the exhaust manifold on the starboard engine, where the heating pipe joined in, was covered over with a metal plate about the size of a man's hand. Carbon monoxide seeped under these plates into the cockpits, Mr Brett-Hilder related. The pilot was always first to succumb, and if his comrades were left with a fighting chance, and tried to climb out the side window of a Beaufort, this was so sited that their feet would have pushed the control column forward and sent the machine into a vertical dive.

Mr Brett-Hilder said this was the official finding of the RAAF court of inquiry in 1943 when investigating the Gippsland death toll. Carbon monoxide was found to be the cause of death. But that finding, he said, was never published.

Who was Mr Brett-Hilder? Well, in 1943 he was a RAAF wing-commander, and *Chairman of That Secret* RAAF *Inquiry Court!*

Index